LOCATION OF INDUSTRY

AND INTERNATIONAL

COMPETITIVENESS

LOCATION OF INDUSTRY AND INTERNATIONAL COMPETITIVENESS

By

SEEV HIRSCH

CLARENDON PRESS
OXFORD
1967

Oxford University Press, Ely House, London W.1

GLASGOW NEW YORK TORONTO MELBOURNE WELLINGTON
CAPE TOWN SALISBURY IBADAN NAIROBI LUSAKA ADDIS ABABA
BOMBAY CALCUTTA MADRAS KARACHI LAHORE DACCA
KUALA LUMPUR HONG KONG TOKYO

PREFACE

This book is based on my doctoral dissertation submitted at the Harvard Graduate School of Business Administration in June 1965.

Many of the ideas discussed originated in 1959, when as a junior economist at the Ministry of Commerce and Industry in Jerusalem I was working in a department which was engaged in evaluating industrial projects. Many of these projects were intended to earn badly needed foreign exchange for the Israeli economy, either directly, by producing goods for export, or indirectly, by producing goods intended to replace imports. It struck me at the time that a systematic analysis of the relationship between the inputs, technology, structure, and marketing activities characterizing different industries might point the way to a limited range of projects which a country might undertake with a reasonable probability of success, given its stage of economic development and its human and natural resources. This type of analysis is attempted in the present book. It seeks to present a view of international competitiveness in terms which are meaningful to those concerned with identifying the competitive potential of different economies and translating this potential into reality.

The book starts by reviewing a number of writings in international trade theory (Chapter I). It then goes on (Chapters II and III) to describe the 'Product-Cycle View of International Competitiveness'. This view is based on the proposition that a country which has a strong competitive position in a given industry at a given time may lose this position when the character of the industry changes—in short, that comparative advantage is not static. The hypothesis proposed is that the comparative advantage a country has in particular industries is determined by the degree of development attained by that country and the maturity of the industries concerned, less developed countries having an advantage in mature industries, industrial leaders in growth products, and small developed countries in new products with a high engineering and scientific content. One relevant factor given special consideration is the effect of export marketing costs on industries of differing maturity.

In the final section of the book (Chapters IV-VI) empirical data —information about the structure and international performance of the United States electronics industry, with special reference to the problems of manufacturing and exporting one particular component, synthetic crystals—are used to assess how far the product-cycle view is consistent with economic reality and helpful as a guide to policy-making. The last chapter considers some implications of this analysis for the formulation of export-promoting and import-replacing policies at the national and the individual firm's level, and examines some of the issues involved in bridging the gap between competitive potential and actual performance.

I wish to record my gratitude to the members of my thesis committee, Professor R. Vernon (chairman), Professor T. Levitt, and Professor E. Shapiro, all of the Harvard Graduate School of Business Administration, for their help and guidance. Their comments, analysis, and sharp criticism helped me to clarify my thoughts and to remove some inconsistencies, and thus led to a thorough revision of the material contained in this book.

Thanks are due to Dr. W. Juda, director of Bolt Beranek and Newman, Inc. of Cambridge, Mass., whose intellectual interest in the possibility of establishing a science-based export-oriented industry in Israel, and willingness to experiment with ideas, spurred me to pursue the subject of this study and enabled me to conduct the field research.

The research was supported by the Harvard University Program on Technology and Society under a long-term grant from the International Business Machines Corporation. The help of the Program is gratefully acknowledged.

Last, but by no means least, I wish to thank my wife who enabled me to have the time and peace of mind required for my work, by taking upon herself the full burden of looking after our family.

Tel Aviv
March 1967   SEEV HIRSCH

CONTENTS

LIST OF FIGURES

I

ECONOMIC THEORY AS A POLICY GUIDE

A. THE NEED FOR POLICY GUIDES

THE purpose of this study is to develop and test an analytical framework, or model, which might be useful for (1) understanding the relationship between the location and international competitiveness of manufacturing industries, (2) formulating policies designed to bridge the gap between the competitive potential of different industries and their actual export performance.

In a classical world of free information, perfect markets, full employment, and absence of friction in the allocation of resources there would be no need for such a framework. Profit, which is a sufficient yardstick of efficiency in this kind of a world, indicates whether the enterprise or the industry under consideration is efficient. In a world of import restriction, tariff protection, and exchange rate manipulations, profits, measured in units of Israeli pounds or Colombian pesos, are not necessarily indicative of whether an Israeli or Colombian enterprise yielding an acceptable profit to its owner is, or is not, using efficiently the country's scarce resources. In the pursuit of given political, social, or economic goals, Governments may institute policies which may, unintentionally, affect the competitiveness and profitability of particular industries.

Textile firms may show satisfactory profits because high customs duties (whose purpose is to raise revenues for the Government) are levied on competing imports, or because the exchange rate at which raw cotton is imported into the country is overvalued. Overvaluation of the national currency may, by the same token, make textile exports unprofitable. Under these circumstances Government policy-makers and businessmen alike need guidelines which would indicate to them whether further expansion of the textile industry is desirable on economic grounds.

Moreover, it is generally agreed that the evaluation of the expected benefits and costs to the economy of industries which have yet to be established cannot possibly be based solely on the projection of balance sheets and income statements, even when the difficulties involved in gathering the information which is needed for making reliable forecasts can somehow be solved. Granting of administrative protection to industries whose immediate profit prospectives may seem remote, might be socially justified even by the reckonings of those economists who do not condone Government intervention in the free flow of trade:

Pigou, Taussig, Viner as well as almost all modern theorists emphasize that it is possible, in principle, to speed the development of individual industries or of industry as a whole through such protectionist measures as import restrictions or subsidies. This will, under suitable conditions, result in their faster development than would be the case if all forces were permitted their free play; as a consequence, at the end of the protective period these industries may enjoy a comparative advantage and be able to meet foreign competition without benefit of protection.[1]

What criteria might be used to determine which industries should be singled out for protection and for the application of other incentives intended to speed their development? G. Haberler suggests that the eventual removal of protection will indicate whether the decision to encourage the establishment of a given industry was a wise one.[2] This *ex post facto* test is indeed useful and welcome if the policy appears to have been a wise one, and the new industry is subsequently able to withstand the test of international competition. However, if the policy turns out to be mistaken, it will be difficult to undo its harmful consequences. The investment made in physical equipment, labour training, transportation facilities, etc. may not be easily transferred to other fields of endeavour because of the specialized nature of the equipment and difficulties involved in transferring skills and aptitudes acquired in one industry to another. Furthermore, vested interests may have been created, and the pressures for maintaining

---

[1] G. von Haberler, 'A Survey of International Trade Theory', *Special Papers in International Economics* No. 1 (Princeton University Press, 1961), p. 56.

[2] Ibid, p. 56. Haberler further states that the ability of an industry to compete without protection constitutes an insufficient justification for employing the policy, since 'against the advantage gained through successful nurturing of an industry must be set the temporary losses in national income sustained during the period of protection'.

established policies even when they turn out to be mistaken are likely to be hard to resist.

A case in point is the decision of the Israel Government to encourage and support the establishment of a local steel industry in the middle nineteen-fifties. While using up scarce resources such as electricity and skilled labour, as well as foreign exchange to import ore, the industry has thus far failed to measure up even remotely to international cost standards. Despite this demonstrable failure, reflected in the high cost of local steel, the Government seems unable to undo the mistake. The political costs of admitting publicly a mistake of such magnitude and of having to cope with the temporary dislocation caused by the dismissal of workers appear to be too high.[1] The controversial decision of the British Government to force the British Overseas Airways Corporation to buy a certain number of VC-10 jet airliners despite their inability to compete internationally shows that the problem of resisting vested interests is not limited to developing countries.[2]

In addition to the infant industry argument discussed above, several other factors inhibit the use of profits as a clear-cut guide to rational decision-making, at least at the national level. A. Hirschman demonstrated in detail the external economies resulting from the forward and backward 'linkage effects' created by certain strategic investments.[3] The benefits accruing to the economy may be present in the form of increased output or efficiency of another plant or industry only remotely connected with the investment project under consideration. Such benefits are not, as a rule, 'internalized' by the individual entrepreneur, because his profit calculus is likely to be different from that of the whole economy. In the absence of special incentives he will not necessarily act in accordance with the national interest.

[1] This account is based on several articles in the Israeli press and on the Industrial Advisory Group study: *First Interim Report on the 'Steel Town' Pig Iron and Steel Project. Israel. An Economic Appraisal* (Jerusalem, Government Printing Office, 1957).

[2] *The Economist* had the following comments on the VC-10 episode; '... It may be the lesser of two evils to make BOAC take the VC-10 now, rather than to bleed the aircraft industry white by cancelling them. But let no one have any illusions about the size of the price which would have to be paid.

'Reprieving the VC-10 comes perilously close to accepting (without exposing the argument and pressing it through) the permanent subsidizing of an international airline in order to provide a captive market for an already subsidized aircraft industry.' 18 July 1964, p. 271.

[3] A. O. Hirschman, *The Strategy of Economic Development* (Yale University Press, 1958).

A gap between social benefits and private costs is liable to exist in all economies. It may be especially wide in less developed countries, where the profitability of whole sectors and industries may be affected by the addition of a road connecting existing plants to newly discovered sources of raw materials, or by building a single power station in a region where electricity was previously unavailable.

Can other criteria replace profits or profit prospects as the yardstick by which it is possible to gauge the long-run competitive potential of different industries? The quest for such guidelines starts with a brief review of some policy prescriptions implicit in writings on international trade theory.

B. COMPARATIVE V. ABSOLUTE ADVANTAGE

According to international trade theory, competitiveness is predicated upon the difference between the ratios at which various goods can be exchanged domestically and in the international market. If in Britain a unit of wheat can be exchanged for two units of cloth, and in the United States a unit of wheat can be exchanged for one unit of cloth, Britain enjoys a comparative advantage in cloth, and the United States a comparative advantage in wheat. Every country has, by definition, a comparative advantage in some products. Even if all production factors are more efficient in the U.S. than in Britain, it will still be profitable for the two countries to sell to each other goods in which they are *relatively* efficient in exchange for others in which they are comparatively inefficient.

Thus comparative rather than absolute advantage makes trade between different countries attractive to all parties, and determines which products will be imported and which will be sold abroad.

And yet, as G. Haberler observed, 'The flow of international trade is determined directly by absolute differences in money prices and not by comparative differences in labor costs'.[1] Haberler has shown how comparative advantage gets translated into absolute cost advantage by means of an elaborate model which took into account productivity, wages, transport costs, demand

---

[1] G. von Haberler, *The Theory of International Trade with its Applications to Commercial Policy* (New York, The Macmillan Co., 1936), p. 131.

patterns, and exchange rates. A simplified numerical example which illustrates his model is reproduced below:

TABLE I(1)

Kind of Goods	A	B	C	D	E	F	G	H	I	J
in country I a1, b1.	20	20	20	20	20	20	20	20	20	20
country II a2, b2.	40	36	32	30	25	20	18	16	14	12

Source: Haberler, *The Theory of International Trade with its Applications to Commerical Policy*, p. 138. A footnote states: 'We choose the units of quantity of the various commodities in such a way that the cost per unit of every commodity in country I is the same. Hence the equality (all costing 20) is not a simplifying assumption.'

The unit costs in local currency in the two countries are given in the body of the table, which ranks the commodities in the order of their competitiveness. The exchange rate between the currencies of the two countries will determine which product will be imported and which will be exported. Given an exchange rate of 1 to 1, for example, country I exports to country II products A to E, since the price of these products (assuming that price equals cost) in country I is cheaper than in country II. The latter exports products G to J in payment for its imports. The exchange rate in turn will be determined by the demand of each country for the products of its trading partner. If no net capital movements take place, the quantity of imports will equal that of exports.

How is this model reflected in the profit and loss statement of an individual firm? A partial answer is suggested by the following equations, which show the variables determining the profitability of exporting from, say, Britain to the United States.

(1) $$Y = C + P$$

(2) $$Y = F \cdot r$$

Y = total receipts in £
C = Total costs of manufacturing in £
P = profits in £
F = total foreign exchange receipts in $
r = exchange rate £/$

Equation (1) is an abbreviated profit and loss statement showing sales to equal costs of manufacturing plus profits.

Equation (2) brings in the foreign exchange element by showing sales to equal foreign exchange receipts F multiplied by the exchange rate r.

Equation (3) is derived by substituting Y in (1) for its equivalent in (2).

$$(3) \qquad\qquad C + P = F \cdot r$$

For profits to be positive, receipts must exceed costs, and the ratio of costs to receipts must be higher than the ratio at which the pound sterling is converted into dollars.[1] In other words the ratio at which the firm converts dollars into pounds (C/F) must be smaller than the ratio at which the whole economy exchanges the two currencies. The smaller the ratio C/F the higher the profit of the firm, and vice versa.

The equations show that a profitable exporter benefits the whole economy because he earns foreign exchange at a low internal conversion rate. Table I(1) contains a clue as to the identity of the profitable exporter. The export of product A from country I seems more profitable than that of products B, C, etc. (see Table I(1)). Should one therefore expect manufacturers of product A to benefit more from exports than the manufacturers of the lower ranking products?

Haberler's model implies that the answer to the question should be affirmative. Considering that the ratio of production costs between countries I and II is 20/40 for product A and 20/36 for product B, the export of the second product might be expected to be *less* profitable than that of the first. This view, however, fails to take into account the demand side of the trade equation. To illustrate this point consider again Table I(1). It is quite possible that the market in country II will fail to absorb additional units of product A at the favourable price of forty units.[2] Demand in country II may be inelastic, and the price of product A may fall as additional units are imported from country I. If, moreover, competition amongst manufacturers of product A is intense, and if the elasticity

[1] $P > 0 \rightarrow C \langle F \cdot r \rightarrow r \rangle C/F$.
Since $r = \pounds/\$$, it follows that $\pounds/\$ > C/F$ as a condition for a positive profit.
[2] The reader is reminded that the exchange rate between the currencies of the two countries is assumed to be $1 = 1$.

of the demand for the product is low, prices may rapidly fall below the level of products B, C, D, and even E. This example indicates that the ranking method implied by Table I(1) can only identify products which are candidates for exports under different exchange rates. The method fails to rank these products according to their potential profitability.

The method presented in Table I(1) suffers from another short-coming; in order to construct such a table, policy-makers must possess detailed technical information about the production function of numerous products which are *not currently* produced domestically, and which may not be produced in the future. They must, moreover, have detailed knowledge about the cost of different production factors and the proportion in which they are employed in the manufacture of all products under consideration. The number of production factors is, however, far smaller than that of products. It would therefore appear that if sufficient information were gathered about the nature, availability, and prices of production factors which the national economy can command, policy-makers would be well placed to identify the industries which might utilize these factors to best advantage. The 'factor-endowment' approach discussed in the following section represents an attempt to explain comparative advantage along these lines.

C. THE HECKSCHER-OHLIN THEOREM AND THE 'LEONTIEF PARADOX'

The 'factor-endowment' or 'factor-proportion' theorem, which was developed by the Swedish economists Heckscher and Ohlin, seeks to explain why individual countries possess a comparative advantage in the export of given products. The essence of the Heckscher-Ohlin theorem, as it was termed, is simply that 'countries tend to export those commodities requiring more of their plentiful factors'.[1] Relative scarcity tends to be reflected in prices, and the products embodying a relatively high proportion of the abundant factors are likely to be less expensive than those containing more of the scarce ones. As trade between nations opens up, a country's exports list will be heavily weighted with products containing a high proportion of its ample factors, and imports will

---

[1] R. E. Caves, *Trade and Economic Structure* (Cambridge, Harvard University Press, 1960), p. 28.

be biased towards items containing a high proportion of scarce factors. The theorem inspired a great deal of debate and criticism, focusing on issues beyond the scope of this study.[1] The concern of this section is with the implications of the theorem for policy making.

The first and most obvious conclusion implied by the theorem is that if a country is amply endowed with natural resources for which foreign demand exists it can benefit from exporting such resources. Being obvious, this conclusion is of little use to policy-makers. J. Hicks commented on its shortcomings as follows:

> Ricardo's Portugal exported wine because she had the 'land' (which in the economic sense includes climate) that is needed for wine production; in our day Egypt's cotton, Iraq's petroleum, Brazil's coffee, and the numerous other cases of specialization upon primary products that one could list, are readily explicable in terms of natural resources. All that, however, is very obvious, it needs no subtle economic reasoning to explain these comparative advantages. The crucial test for the factors-scarcity theory (and indeed, as we have seen, for any international trade theory) is to explain the advantage of the industrialized countries. And on that side the factor-scarcity theory is not too successful.[2]

The failure of the theorem to provide an adequate explanation for the competitive advantage which industrialized nations appear to possess in different industries was dramatically illustrated by the so-called 'Leontief Paradox'.

When W. Leontief tried to test the factor-proportion theorem empirically he found, somewhat to his surprise, that the structure of what he termed the U.S. 'export' and 'import-competing' industries was quite different from that which one might expect to observe on the basis of the Heckscher-Ohlin model.[3] Using data available from the 1947 inter-sectoral study of the United States economy, Leontief calculated the capital and labour requirements for the production of $1,000,000 of exports and import-competing goods. His findings indicated that the manufacture of U.S. exports required a *higher* proportion of labour to capital than the manufacture of 'import-competing goods'. The calculation showed

---

[1] See ibid. for a detailed summary of the literature written on the Heckscher-Ohlin theorem.

[2] J. R. Hicks, 'International Trade—The long View' (*Central Bank of Egypt Lectures*, Cairo, Central Bank of Egypt, 1963), p. 6.

[3] W. W. Leontief, 'Domestic Productions and Foreign Trade: The American Capital Position Re-examined,' *Proceedings of the American Philosophical Society*, (1953).

that in order to produce $1,000,000 of exports, U.S. industry needed $2,550,780 of capital and 182,313 man-years of direct and indirect labour. Export industries thus required a capital stock of $14,010 per employee. To produce import-competing goods worth $1,000,000, $3,091,339 of capital and 170,004 man-years were needed. Capital requirements per employee in import-competing industries amounted to $18,180. This figure exceeded investments per employee in the export industries by 30 per cent or nearly $4,200.

Since the U.S. has been traditionally regarded as a country abundantly endowed with capital, these findings clearly conflicted with the expectations of the Heckscher-Ohlin model. These findings, later termed the 'Leontief Paradox', aroused a great deal of comment and controversy in the economic literature.[1] Leontief's methodology, assumptions, and figures were questioned and subjected to criticism by numerous people. Leontief himself was not satisfied with his findings and recalculated the figures several times, using refined data and different methods.[2] The outcome was never substantially different, though later calculations showed that the difference between the capital/labour ratios in the two industry groups was not as marked as the original study indicated.

A subsequent study conducted by Japanese economists on the comparative capital intensity of export and import-competing industries in Japan indicated that Leontief's paradox is not confined to the U.S. The study showed that exports from capital-scarce Japan were, on the average, more capital-intensive than products which had to compete with substantial imports in the local markets.[3]

Two conflicting conclusions of interest to the subject of this study emerge from the findings of Leontief and Tatemoto and Ichimura: Leontief, trying to reconcile his findings with the factor-proportion approach, concluded that, contrary to earlier expectations, the U.S. is indeed a labour-intensive country. The quality of

[1] A bibliography of the literature concerning the Leontief paradox may be found in S. Burenstam-Linder, *An Essay on Trade and Transformation* (Stockholm, Almquist and Wiksell, 1961), p. 84.

[2] W. W. Leontief, 'Factor Proportions and the Structure of American Trade; Further Theoretical and Empirical Analysis,' *Review of Economics and Statistics* (November 1956).

[3] Tatemoto, M., Ichimura, S., 'Factor Proportions and Foreign Trade—The Case of Japan', *Review of Economics and Statistics* (November 1959).

U.S. labour makes up for its relatively small quantity and increases productivity to such an extent that labour is relatively abundant in relation to capital.[1] Leontief's explanation, while preserving the form of the factor-proportion approach, changes its contents. The approach assumes homogeneous production factors, and Leontief changes this assumption by redefining U.S. and foreign labour as different factors of production.

C. Kindleberger, on the other hand, concludes that the Heckscher-Ohlin theorem is incorrect.[2] His criticism is directed against the theorem's assumption of similar production functions in different countries. A given product is likely, according to Kindleberger, to be produced by different combinations of labour and capital in the U.S. than in other countries. Thus, while export goods may be more labour-intensive than import-competing goods, when both are produced in the U.S., the intensities (i.e. relative proportions) may be different elsewhere. Kindleberger's point is well taken. Numerous productive activities are indeed conducted by entirely dissimilar methods in different countries. Rice-growing in the U.S. is highly mechanized, for example. Specialized equipment has been developed to plant the seedlings, to irrigate the fields, and to harvest the crop. In Java, Burma, Japan, and other countries most of these activities are still carried out by human labour, assisted occasionally by draft animals. Other activities such as home-building, vegetable-oil processing, &c. are similarly much more capital-intensive in the advanced economies than in the developing ones.

However, it must be remembered that technological constraints, quality control, and cost considerations often limit industrial production processes within fairly narrow bounds. Mechanical looms are so much more efficient than handweaving that the latter method can be used competitively only where human labour is considered to be practically a free good. It is therefore quite likely that similar methods are employed by textile manufacturers in most countries. The same is probably true of a large number of other processes such as oil-refining and even steel-making.

---

[1] It should be noted that U.S. labour productivity in this context is said to be high not because it is combined with a large quantity of capital, but because of the skills, mental attitudes, and physical fitness which U.S. labour allegedly possesses.

[2] C. P. Kindleberger, *Foreign Trade and the National Economy* (Yale University Press, 1962), p. 77.

E. Robinson stated the same point somewhat differently:

The number of bananas that could be produced by the labor required to build a locomotive would be widely different in Scotland and in the Canary Islands. But as regards a fairly considerable range of standard machine-produced products, it may be doubted whether the differences of relative efficiency are great. Goods are made in different countries with the help of almost identical machines.[1]

Assuming that internationally-traded manufacturers are mostly of the variety belonging to the latter group, can the Leontief paradox be explained while retaining the Heckscher-Ohlin assumption regarding the similarity of the production functions? Leontief hints at an answer in a subsequent article, written in 1956, three years after the publication of his original study.[2] In the article he presents a table showing labour inputs in export and import-competing industries broken down by skill levels. The figures reproduced below in Table I(2) show that the export industries

TABLE I(2)

Relative Employment Costs in the Manufacturing of
Export and Import-Competing Industries in the U.S.

	Export	
Level of skills	*Man-years*	*% of total*
I. Professional, technical, and managerial	23,867	13.75
II. Clerical, sales, services	38,307	22.07
III. Craftsmen and foremen	26,298	15.15
IV. Operatives	52,158	30.05
V. Labourers	32,941	18.98
	173,571	100.00
	Import-competing	
I. Professional, technical, and managerial	19,395	12.24
II. Clerical, sales, services	26,954	17.00
III. Craftsmen and foremen	18,696	11.79
IV. Operatives	44,992	28.38
V. Labourers	48,494	30.59
	158,531	100.00

Source: Leontief, loc. cit.

[1] E. A. G. Robinson, *The Structure of Competitive Industry* (The University of Chicago Press, 1962), p. 144.
[2] W. W. Leontief, 'Factor Proportions and the Structure of American Trade; Further Theoretical and Empirical Analysis', *Review of Economics and Statistics* (November 1956).

employ a higher proportion of skilled labourers than the import-competing industries. Leontief notes this difference in inputs and comments:

> As should have been expected, the relative excess of man-years incorporated in one million dollars worth of U.S. exports over the quantity of labor absorbed in the production of an equivalent amount of domestic goods competing with foreign imports is definitely concentrated in the higher skills. The lowest, i.e., unskilled, category taken by itself shows, as a matter of fact, percentagewise a quite large surplus on the import side.

Leontief does not elaborate as to why he expects a high proportion of skilled manpower to be employed in the export industry. This point, however, may suggest how the Leontief paradox and the Heckscher-Ohlin theorem may be reconciled. Instead of defining U.S. labour as a different production factor from foreign labour, as Leontief did, could one not view different skills as different factors of production? If the five levels of skills referred to in the table were regarded as different factors of production (while retaining the assumption of homogeneity of similar factors in different countries), Leontief's empirical findings could be said to be at least partially consistent with the factor-proportion theorem.

Of the five levels of skill into which the work force was divided, the three highest grades account for nearly 50 per cent of total man-years in exports versus only 40 per cent in import-competing goods. This statistic suggests that the country which has a relatively low wage differential between skilled and unskilled labour will benefit from a comparative cost advantage in the manufacture of products containing a high proportion of skilled labour inputs. Leontief's findings may be reinterpreted as follows: the international competitiveness of U.S. exports can be ascribed at least in part to the relative abundance of skilled labour. This factor could outweigh the relatively little use by the export industries of the country's other abundant resource—capital.

This interpretation of the factor-proportion approach does not affect the policy guidelines implicit in the Heckscher-Ohlin theorem; a country should give priority to the manufacture of products containing a high proportion of locally abundant factors. Factors, however, should be carefully defined in order to avoid possible confusion arising from erroneous classification.

The discussion thus far has emphasized production factors and production costs as the elements which determine comparative advantage. Other factors such as demand patterns and information flows, which similarly affect the volume and composition of international trade, have not been considered. The importance of these factors is stressed and their impact on trade analysed by S. Burenstam-Linder, whose trade model is considered in the following section.

D. S. BURENSTAM-LINDER'S EXPLANATION OF THE COMPOSITION OF TRADE

S. Burenstam-Linder's point of departure is entirely different from the one assumed by the more orthodox economists. He maintains that 'The range of exportable products is determined by internal demand'. And he continues: 'It is a necessary but not a sufficient condition that a product be consumed (or invested) in the home country for this product to be a potential export product'.[1] The writer cites lack of familiarity with foreign markets as the factor responsible for this state of affairs. Lack of familiarity has several aspects. In the first place, entrepreneurs undertake to manufacture a product in response to needs of which they must be aware. In a world of imperfect knowledge, their attention is likely to be drawn mainly to needs which arise at home. This point was forcefully stated by C. Kindleberger:

A man may be perfectly rational but only within a limited horizon. As consumer he will normally restrict his expenditure to those goods offered to him through customary channels. As producer, he will sell his goods typically in a given ambit. Over his horizon there may lie brilliant opportunities to improve his welfare as a consumer, or his income as a producer, but unless he is made aware of them, they will avail him nothing.[2]

To the extent that a product has to be invented, or at least developed from scratch, another aspect of familiarity assumes a degree of importance; the familiarity of the inventor and developer with market requirements. Inventors, like entrepreneurs, do not operate in a vacuum, and they too respond to perceived needs. Lack of knowledge about foreign needs limits the response of the inventors to needs and opportunities which they perceive in the domestic market.

[1] S. Burenstam-Linder, *Essay on Trade and Transformation.*
[2] Kindleberger, *Foreign Trade and the National Economy*, p. 16.

Finally, it is important to realize that products are hardly ever introduced initially into the market in their final form. Prototypes are modified as a result of back and forth exchanges between the manufacturer and the customers. Only after a prolonged period is the product finally introduced on a full commercial scale. The costs of modifications will be much more expensive if the manufacturer is unfamiliar with the market, or if the market is physically or economically remote. After the new product has been firmly established in the domestic market, the entrepreneur is ready to respond to profit opportunities in foreign markets. Once products have been sold abroad there is, of course, no reason why exports should not account for a major share of total output. Only rarely will this sequence be reversed and foreign sales precede the development of the domestic market or even coincide with it, according to Burenstam-Linder.

Having concluded that the list of potential exportable products is contingent upon the existence of a domestic market, Burenstam-Linder points out that the patterns of domestic demand are influenced to an important degree by income. Income, more than any other variable, appears to determine the consumption and purchasing habits of broad sectors of the population. Countries having similar income levels are consequently likely to trade with each other more intensively than countries having different income levels. Comparative advantage, in summary, is a condition brought about not by objective economic forces such as factor endowment but by a mixture of historic accidents and the conscious activities of entrepreneurs. This fact does not make the comparative advantage less real or even less stable than it is assumed to be according to the Heckscher-Ohlin theorem:

Through the division of labor, natural skills will develop and be strengthened in fields that have become typical of each country. An emerging pattern of trade will affect the future environment of investors and innovators, the efforts of which will be channelled differently in the various countries. Economies of scale will assert themselves. Habit-forming brand advertising will cement the consumption pattern. These forces will gradually create a gap between what might originally have been almost identical prices and eventually make a fragile pattern of comparative advantage more substantial.[1]

Burenstam-Linder's essay is intended to be descriptive rather than to prescribe modes of action. Implicitly, however, his model

[1] Ibid., p. 196.

contains certain guidelines of which both Government planners and individual firms might take cognizance. The first concerns the timing of international trade activities; the sooner firms raise their trade horizons across national boundaries, the more likely they are to benefit from economies of scale and from all the other benefits derived from higher sales volumes. The second guideline concerns the directions of export endeavours: these should be concentrated on countries whose average income level is roughly equal to that of the exporting country.

These conclusions, it should be observed, are diametrically opposed to the policy recommendations indicated by the Heckscher-Ohlin theorem, which implicitly assumes that trade between capital-rich and capital-poor countries tends to be more promising for the trading partners than exchange of goods between countries whose average income levels are similar, where labour and capital may be expected to be distributed in similar proportions.

An alternative approach which contains elements from both approaches discussed above while introducing a number of additional variables into the analysis of international competitiveness is presented in the following chapters.

II

INTERNATIONAL COMPETITIVENESS: THE PRODUCTION FUNCTION

A. THE PRODUCT-CYCLE APPROACH

THE analytical approach discussed in this chapter proceeds from the empirical observation that industries and individual products undergo several important changes over time. Sales volume, production methods, factor inputs, prices, and other economic elements which characterize a given product during its introductory phase appear to assume different magnitudes, relative importance, and weights as the product enters more mature phases. The approach developed in this chapter is based on the premise that these changes occur in a fairly systematic fashion, and are therefore predictable.

S. Kuznets, who investigated in detail the long-term developments of thirty-five industries, found that when the sales volume of an industry was plotted on a chart it almost invariably conformed to the pattern described by Figure 1. His observations led him to conclude that:

A rapidly developing industry does not retain its vigorous growth forever but slackens and is overtaken by others whose period of rapid development is beginning. Within one country we can observe a succession of different branches of activity in the vanguard of the country's economic development, and within each industry we can notice a conspicuous slackening in the rate of increase.[1]

The phases through which many products typically pass are illustrated in Figure 1. Time is indicated on the horizontal axis and sales volume is shown on the vertical axis. As new products are first introduced into the market, sales tend to be low. While the rate at which sales rise may be increasing, total volume remains relatively

[1] S. Kuznets, *Economic Change* (New York, W. W. Norton & Co., 1953), p. 254.

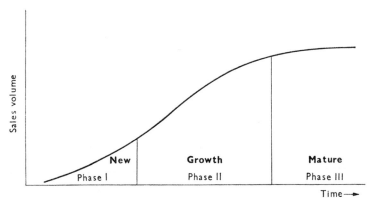

Figure 1
The Product-Cycle Curve

modest throughout the first phase. A sharp increase in volume characterizes the second phase. Growth rate, which is comparatively high at the beginning of the second phase, tends to slacken towards its latter part. The curve flattens out in the third phase, and may either continue on a plateau or decline, depending on whether the product in question is replaced or continues to be bought.

The division of the cycle into three separate phases is of course quite arbitrary. A different subdivision into fewer phases (mature *v.* new, for example) or a larger number of phases might be equally plausible. For the present purpose, the division of the cycle into three phases was considered most useful because it facilitates the consideration of the product-cycle approach in sufficient detail without over-simplifying the analysis.

Before proceeding with a detailed discussion of the first phase, it might be desirable to define the term 'new product'. Several definitions of the term are of course possible. A product might, for example, be considered new if it embodied raw materials which were developed only recently. Other definitions may emphasize the production process, the end use, &c. The definition used here is that of Kuznets, who defined new products as involving a 'revolutionary invention or discovery' which 'changed the industrial process fundamentally'.[1] Kuznets's definition focuses on

[1] Ibid., p. 259.

the technology used in the production process. A product is considered new if (1) it is manufactured by methods which were not previously used by the industry, and (2) it is based on a recent invention or unfamiliar developments.

By this definition new cars, though they replace old models, are not considered new products. Transistor radios and jet aeroplanes on the other hand did qualify as new products when they were introduced into the market in the middle fifties, despite the fact that radios and aeroplanes were first developed several decades previously. The relevance of this definition will become clearer in the following pages, where the economic characteristics of new and mature products are discussed.

The introductory phase of the product cycle is usually characterized by high unit costs and a labour-intensive production function. Though the product has gone past the pilot production stage, many 'bugs' are still present in the production process. Runs are short, and the product is frequently manufactured in individual units or in relatively small batches. Manufacture by assembly-line methods or continuous processes is comparatively rare at this stage.[1] Product specifications are loose, and frequent changes are introduced into the manufacturing process, production sequence, product specification, and equipment.

In order to minimize the costs involved in coping with the problems caused by the inherent instability of the production process, manufacturers try to keep their investments in fixed assets and fixed overheads down as far as possible. They refrain from installing special-purpose machinery which is more suitable for turning out long runs of standardized products. Rather than operate their own specialized equipment, testing facilities, ancillary services, &c., manufacturers of new products tend to rely on sub-contractors and independent specialist firms to perform for them a large number of manufacturing operations and services. Consequently the efficiency and flexibility of firms producing new or first-phase products can be considerably enhanced if sub-contractors, suppliers, and firms providing specialized services are easily accessible, and if communication with them can be readily

---

[1] Chemicals and petrochemicals are examples of products which may be produced by continuous processes as soon as they are commercially available. Even in these cases, however, the scale of the production unit is usually comparatively small at the outset.

maintained. The terms on which these 'external economies'[1] are available to the producers determine to an important extent their costs, and the range of products which they are able to manufacture on a competitive basis.

New products contain a high proportion of scientific and engineering inputs. Professional knowledge and experience are most critical for their successful development and their ability to survive the introductory phase. The employment costs of engineers and scientists are therefore likely to account for a higher proportion of total outlays during the early phase than in any other phase of the cycle. The ability of individuals and teams of scientists and/or engineers to cope with the problems which are encountered during the early phase is probably the single most important determinant of success.

Entry into the market is limited by know-how rather than by financial considerations. Patent rights or possession of specialized skills protect the pioneer against encroachment from newcomers. Capital requirements are comparatively modest, owing to the nature of the production function discussed above. The absolute amount of capital required to enter the automobile industry in the early twenties was, for example, considerably smaller than the amount needed forty years later, even after due allowance has been made for price changes.

It is more difficult to generalize about the pricing and marketing aspects of new products, though certain general remarks appear to be called for. W. Salter suggests that 'Even though methods and techniques may be very crude, it is often economic to begin production almost immediately, because a high price may be charged'.[2] The price history of nylon, polyethylene, transistors, radios, television sets, automobiles, and numerous other products confirms this observation, indicating that prices of most products are indeed highest during the early phases of their introduction to the market.

Lack of competition, and the necessity to pay for development and experimentation with different production methods, designs,

[1] The present usage of the term 'external economies' is based on M. Hall (ed.), *Made in New York* (Cambridge, Harvard University Press, 1963). This study contains several detailed examples which show how the location of industry in the New York metropolitan region has been affected by the availability of external economies.

[2] W. E. G. Salter, *Productivity and Technical Change* (Cambridge University Press, 1960), p. 133.

and materials, explain this phenomenon from the seller's point of view. Demand in turn will depend on the availability, performance, and quality of substitutes. As long as a new product fulfils a given need better than an existing substitute, the public may be expected to pay for it at least as much as it did for the existing product, and possibly even more. When, consequently, a new item can be manufactured more cheaply than the one it is intended to displace, manufacturers may make substantial profits during the introductory phases, until competition catches up with them and forces prices down closer to the level of production costs.

Products that survive the introductory stage next enter the growth phase, during which mass production and mass distribution are introduced. Production runs are lengthened, and special-purpose machinery may be utilized to reduce unit costs. Assembly-line methods, continuous processes, and other mass production techniques are introduced whenever possible. The ratio of labour to capital is consequently reduced, and the production process becomes more capital-intensive.

An increasing number of firms are attracted to the industry to take advantage of a growing market. The expiry of patents, the development of close substitutes, and the acquisition of manufacturing skills makes entry technically possible. Suppliers of venture capital interested in backing enterprises possessing capabilities in expanding markets make entry possible even in fields requiring heavy capital investments. Casualties are also mounting, since many of the entrants are ill-equipped to serve the market competitively.

Demand is becoming more elastic as far as the individual producer is concerned, since customers have a larger number of suppliers to choose from. In order to attract customers and maintain their market share, manufacturers have to offer services not available before, such as fast delivery, extended breakdown guarantee, and repair facilities.

In this phase skills of administration, of cost control, and of imaginative marketing methods assume critical importance for the firm. Management, defined in the broadest sense of the word, becomes the single most important human input.

As the market gets saturated, the product enters the mature phase. Industry sales volume reaches a plateau, though market shares of individual firms may vary. Product specifications are by now quite standardized. The sequence of operations and their scale are more or less fixed, and innovations in either the product or the production process are getting rarer with maturity.

The manufacturing process becomes more capital-intensive than in the previous phases, and the optimal size of the manufacturing unit becomes larger. Consequently, economies of scale become an important factor in determining the competitive strength of individual manufacturers.

The composition of the labour force changes; the proportion of unskilled and semi-skilled workers rises in comparison with previous phases, and their employment costs account for a growing percentage of the wage bill.

The number of firms in the industry is not changing much from year to year, though dropouts tend to outnumber new entrants. Firms entering the field tend to be large. Entry is commonly achieved through merger and acquisition rather than by the establishment of new organizations. Exit, in turn, becomes very costly, since the specialized equipment and manufacturing processes can rarely be used to produce other products without substantial modifications.

Demand is becoming more and more price-sensitive. Prices have to be adjusted to the level of the least expensive seller. Customer expectations regarding the products, their specifications, prices, and useful life expectancy become stable, as do their buying habits. They are well informed about alternative sources of supply and sufficiently experienced to differentiate between diverging qualities.

Kuznets summarizes the transition of products from the new to the mature stage as follows:

While the stimulus for further invention appears early, the number of operations to be improved is limited and is gradually exhausted. When all the important operations are performed by machines that have reached comparative perfection, not much room is left for further inventions ... This gradual exhaustion of the protracted 'industrial revolution' is accompanied and furthered by the weakening of the economic stimulus. When the reduced price of a commodity has taken it out of the luxury class, a low unit price renders the demand for it largely inelastic, and further possible reductions are too slight to have any marked effect.[1]

Few elements of the model outlined in these pages can be regarded at this stage as proven. The major premises on which it is

---

[1] Kuznets, op. cit., p. 266.

built ought to be viewed as comprising a series of hypotheses which have yet to be tested empirically before they can be accepted as representing economic reality. Some empirical evidence gleaned from published material is presented in the remaining section of this chapter and in Chapter III. More detailed data, representing the writer's own research, is discussed in detail in Chapters IV and V. At this stage the reader is being asked to consider the product-cycle approach as a tool which might be helpful in analysing and evaluating certain product and industry characteristics which are a function of time rather than of physical properties, price, or end use. He might also bear in mind that the validity of the approach and its usefulness for formulating market strategy have been recognized by academic writers and business practitioners alike. Elements of this approach are found in articles written about numerous products ranging from nylon[1] and building materials[2] to television.[3]

The following paragraph, which describes the history of the radio industry, shows how the general model developed here is in accord with the cycle of a particular industry:

In the 1920's that industry had all the earmarks of an activity whose establishments were heavily dependent on external economies, speed and personal contact. Its technology was unsettled and changing rapidly; its production methods were untried, its market was uncertain. Accordingly, at that stage, producers were typically small in size, numerous, agile, nervous, heavily reliant upon sub-contractors and suppliers. Mortality in the industry was high. A decade or two later, however, the technology of the industry had settled down. Production methods were standardized and sets were being turned out in long runs. Now, the critical competitive question had become transport and labor costs, rather than product design. The small firm faded from the picture and large assembly plants appeared at lower-wage locations more centrally placed for national markets. An industry which once was in the external-economy category had evidently changed its nature.[4]

The major points covered in the present section are summarized in Table II(1), which shows how factors such as the production

[1] J. P. Jordan, 'Yale, The Strategy of Nylon's Growth, Creative New Markets', *Modern Textiles Magazine* (February 1964).
[2] C. F. Rassweiler, 'Product Strategy and Future Profits', *Research Review* (April 1961).
[3] A. Patton, 'Top Management Stake in a Product's Life Cycle', in T. L. Berg and A. Shuchman (eds.), *Product Strategy and Management* (Holt, Rinehart and Winston, Inc., 1963).
[4] H. Vernon and E. Hoover, *Metropolis, 1985* (Harvard University Press, 1963).

TABLE II(1)

Characteristics of the Product Cycle

Characteristics	Cycle Phase		
	Early	*Growth*	*Mature*
Technology	short runs. rapidly changing techniques. dependence on external economies.	mass production methods gradually introduced. variations in techniques still frequent.	long runs and stable process. few innovations of importance.
Capital Intensity	low.	high, due to high obsolescence rate.	high, due to large quantity of specialized equipment.
Industry Structure	entry is know-how determined. numerous firms.	growing number of firms. many casualties and mergers. growing integration.	market position and financial resources affect entry. number of firms declining.
Critical Human Inputs	scientific and engineering.	management.	unskilled and semiskilled labour.
Demand Structure	sellers' market. performance and price of substitutes determine buyers' expectations.	individual producers face growing price-elasticity. competition reducing prices. product information spreading.	buyers' market. information easily available.

process, conditions of entry, industry and demand structure, &c. vary from one phase of the cycle to the other.

The following sections examine the relationship between a country's stage of development and factor endowment on the one hand, and its ability to manufacture competitively products passing through different phases of the cycle on the other.

B. THE MATURE PHASE—AN OPPORTUNITY FOR DEVELOPING COUNTRIES

When a developing country embarks upon the road to industrialization, a choice has to be made regarding the kind of industry which the country should build. The guidance which policy-makers can expect from economic theory has been discussed earlier. Presently, the product-cycle model introduced in the last section is brought to bear upon problems of industrial development.

It might be observed, to start with, that in the process of industrialization the establishment of a textile industry usually precedes that of most others. In Japan, India, several Latin-American countries, many of the new African nations, &c., textile plants historically lead the march towards industrialization. How can this phenomenon be explained? A follower of the factor-proportion approach might explain that textiles are relatively labour-intensive and that a capital-poor country may therefore expect to develop a comparative advantage in this field. The following passage represents this view: 'Generally in clothing the labour costs element is an important part of total cost and this makes the industry a particularly appropriate one for establishing in the relatively underdeveloped countries which have a large potential labor force, and where wages are relatively low'.[1]

Burenstam-Linder's approach suggests a different explanation: textiles are first on the industrialization schedule because a local market for the industry's output exists in practically every country. The manufacturer does not have to overcome the obstacles posed by distance in order to market his output. Demand can be easily ascertained and output planned accordingly. These factors, combined with the nature of the manufacturing process, give domestic

[1] S. J. Wells, *British Export Performance—A Comparative Study* (Cambridge University Press, 1964).

producers in the developing countries an important advantage over external competitors, and enable them to maintain a strong competitive position in their domestic markets.

A third explanation is offered by the product-cycle model. The textile industry is a mature one and can therefore be easily transplanted to new environments. The production process is stable and well established. The sequence of operations is strictly specified and leaves comparatively little room for mistakes (or even initiative for that matter). Machinery is standardized, easily obtainable and maintainable. For these reasons it is a relatively simple matter to train even poorly-educated labourers to tend the machines and to manufacture products of acceptable quality. A few people possessing specialized skills and experience are needed to man certain key positions in the plant. These may be drawn from the local *élite*, or, if necessary, may be imported from abroad. The great majority of the operators can always be hired locally. Strict product specifications, the availability of machinery which operates at a predetermined sequence and tolerance, and above all, the suitability of unskilled labour to the manufacturing process combine thus to facilitate the early introduction of the textile industry into industrializing economies.

The three approaches presented here are all plausible, and, since they do not mutually exclude each other, they may all be 'correct'. This happy state of affairs, however, cannot be sustained when other industries are considered. Take the steel industry, for example. The factor-proportion approach will reject the idea of establishing the industry in developing countries on the grounds that it is capital-intensive and therefore too costly for capital-poor countries. A follower of Burenstam-Linder's approach will link his approval of the establishment of the industry in, say, India to the existence of a substantial demand for steel products in that country. The product-cycle approach suggests that steel is a sensible candidate for a country like India, since the steel industry is a mature one. The production function is, as in the case of textiles, stable and strictly specified in the sense that it does not vary from country to country. The degrees of freedom available to the scheduling and design engineers are rather limited. The labour force, though more skilled than textile workers, can be trained with relative ease. The number of highly qualified key personnel is comparatively small. If certain other conditions such as availability of raw materials and the existence of a sufficiently large market to facilitate the operation of optimum-size plants are satisfied, there is no reason why steel should be excluded from the list of industries suitable for industrializing countries.[1] Possession of a steel industry is considered in many countries as a national objective whose desirability cannot be measured in terms of conventional cost and profitability yardsticks. Governments have, moreover, at their disposal numerous measures which can be used to subsidize local industries in ways which will effectively disguise their inefficiency. Available information indicates, nevertheless, that Indian steel, for example, costs less than competitive imports. Moreover, the production processes used by Indian steel producers are practically identical to those used in capital-rich countries such as Britain.

G. Rosen, who studied the Indian steel industry, noted with regard to the first point that while Indian steel users pay an identical price for locally produced and imported steel local manufacturers in fact subsidize the importers. Steel producers get for their output a retention price which is considerably lower than the sales price paid by the customers: 'The difference between the two prices is paid by the company to a government equalization fund which is used to make up the difference between the price of imported steel and the fixed domestic price.'[2]

Regarding the production process, Rosen quoted one estimate which showed the gross fixed capital per worker in steel to be somewhat higher in India than in the U.K. The comparative figures were 48,678 rupees in the U.K. and 54,011 rupees in the works of the Indian Tata Steel Company. Commenting on the new Government-owned steel plants being installed, Rosen noted that: 'There will be a capital labor coefficient in the government plants of 117,000 rupees per worker, or over double the average fixed capital per worker figures for both TISCO [Tata Iron and Steel

---

[1] It may be noted in passing that Albert O. Hirschman too is in favour of establishing a steel industry, though for different reasons. He is favourably impressed by the 'linkage effects' which a steel industry will help to create. Several ancillary industries and services such as electrical plants, refractory materials, improved transportation facilities, &c. will have to be established in order to support the steel industry. Moreover, pressure will be created for the establishment of steel-using industries such as pipes, building materials, shipbuilding, &c. See Hirschman, *The Strategy of Economic Development*.

[2] G. Rosen, 'Industrial Change in India', *Case Studies in Economic Development* (MIT, Centre for International Studies, The Free Press of Glencoe, 1958), p. 73.

Co.] and the British Industry.'[1] The economic soundness of the policy of using capital-intensive production methods in industry in countries such as India is defended by Rosen on the grounds that:

...The scarcities of specific types of labor, skilled and semi-skilled, trained technicians and engineers—make the notion of 'unlimited' labor supply a hollow one to the industrialist: at the same time, the costs of assembling and training a labor force, and the lower productivity of this labor force... contribute to making industrial labor costly in both money and real terms.[2]

Another example of a capital-intensive industry which is often located in developing countries is that of oil-refining. Despite the high capital investment required and the necessity of employing numerous high-cost foreign technicians, oil companies often find it advantageous to locate their refineries in the developing countries. The calculus of transportation and distribution costs (as well as political prudence, admittedly) gives credence to the claim that refineries located near the source of the oil make good economic sense even when the bulk of the output is intended for export rather than for local consumption. It is quite likely that if refining required high inputs of labour—both skilled and unskilled—oil could not be economically refined in places such as Abadan, Ras Tanura, or Tripoli.

Chemical fertilizers and petrochemicals furnish additional examples of capital-intensive industries which are operating successfully in capital-poor countries. No general claim can be made about their competitiveness. The mere fact that they exist, whereas numerous less capital-intensive industries do not, supports the premises of the product-cycle approach.

The successful introduction of mature industries into developing countries may be aided by the very fact that they reached the mature stage in the developed economies. Faced with stagnant demand and falling prices at home, firms in the industry are looking for opportunities to utilize their excess physical and managerial capacity abroad. This may be achieved through the export of know-how and equipment, in the form of direct investment. Alternatively, idle equipment may be sold abroad and engineers may accept offers of foreign employment. G. Baldwin, who made a detailed study of industrial development in southern

---

[1] Ibid., p. 138.   [2] Ibid., p. 147.

India, observed for example that 'A not uncommon arrangement among Bangalore firms was for Indian entrepreneurs to undertake the manufacture of a product according to the specification of, and under licence from, an established foreign firm. . . . In many cases, a few foreign production men set up and started the factory.'[1]

The fact that the exported equipment is often obsolete from the point of view of the exporting country tends to reduce its cost considerably, thus lowering the cost of capital to the importer. Numerous examples of investment projects motivated, at least in part, by the opportunity of exporting unused production equipment abroad may be cited. A case study entitled *Ecuadorian Rubber Company*, which is based on the actual experience of a U.S. rubber company operating in Ecuador, describes a situation where a company received a large share in the equity of an Ecuadorian tyre producer in return for making second-hand equipment available to the joint venture.[2] Another example is provided by the Pacific Vegetable Oil Company of San Francisco, which entered into serious negotiations with the Indonesian Government on the establishment of a copra oil plant in Indonesia on the assumption that its major contribution to the venture would consist of idle production equipment.[3]

In summary, the early establishment of textile industries in many industrializing countries is not only to be explained by the labour intensity of the production process and the existence of a home market. An additional and significant factor is the maturity of the industry and the stability of the production process, which must be easily exportable. An industrializing country may be competitive in the manufacture of mature products even when they are capital-intensive, because the cost of capital may be less important than that of other factors. The administrative skills of management, the ability to adjust the manufacturing process at short notice, the capacity to manoeuvre quickly a complex organization are all more heavily taxed in the case of less mature industries. There is a trade-off between the higher costs of capital and

[1] G. B. Baldwin, 'Industrial Growth in South India', *Case Studies in Economic Development* (MIT, Centre for International Studies, The Free Press of Glencoe, 1960), p. 329.
[2] Harvard Graduate School of Business Administration, *Ecuadorian Rubber Co.*, ICH 9G103.
[3] Harvard Graduate School of Business Administration, *Pacific Vegetable Oil Corporation*, ICH 9G101.

those of obtaining or training better-skilled management and labour. The trade-off may at times favour the capital-intensive but mature industry over the labour-intensive new industry.[1]

Industrialization of developing economies may be viewed in part as a process of gradually extending the range of local production capabilities by establishing industries which are less mature than those already in existence. As technical experience and management skills are acquired and digested, the establishment of newer industries becomes economically feasible. Graphically, the process may be described as the extension of the range of industrial activities leftwards along the product-cycle curve depicted in Figure 1. Developing economies start the industrialization process by establishing industries located at the north-east corner of the curve. The process continues by a westward movement along the curve as newer industries are gradually established with each passing period.

C. THE GROWTH PHASE—THE INDUSTRIAL LEADERS' STRONGEST ADVANTAGE

The second phase of the cycle is the phase during which products begin to enter the stage of mass production, mass distribution, and mass consumption. It is contended here that it is in this phase rather than in the mature one that the industrial leaders such as the United States have the biggest advantage. The reasons for this claim have already been hinted at in the previous section. The skills of organization and of frequent adjustment of the production process, and the ability to combine mass production methods with non-uniform outputs, are most crucial at this stage. Using the language of the Heckscher-Ohlin theorem, it might be said that the U.S. is well endowed with the production factors which are most needed during the second phase of the product cycle.

These expectations appear to be confirmed by a study of U.S. export performance reported by Hal B. Lary.[2] The author

---

[1] Baldwin notes for example that 'Where foreign firms and Indians participated jointly in establishing a new enterprise, the most important contribution of the foreigner was not his capital but his labor, especially at the managerial level and at the level of skilled workmen...', op. cit.

[2] *Problems of the United States as World Trader and Banker* (National Bureau of Economic Research, Princeton University Press, 1963).

divided the country's exports into groups which improved their performance over the 1953–6 period and those which experienced a decline. Among the manufactures belonging to the former group, Lary lists aircraft engines, construction and mining machinery, capital equipment, and electrical machinery. The stagnant or declining group includes iron and steel-mill products, petroleum, tractors, trucks and buses, automobiles, textile manufactures, pharmaceuticals, and consumer appliances.[1]

The items belonging to the first group require a high proportion of engineering and skilled labour inputs. Though they are produced in relatively large numbers they are not as a rule mass-produced; they are, in short, products belonging to the second phase of the cycle. The list of declining exports is made up largely of mature products which have long entered the mass production stage.[2]

Lary provides a partial explanation for the decline of exports in the second group:

...Europe has lagged badly behind the U.S. in the development of continuous strip mills, and sheet steel production was until very recently inadequate to meet the needs of the booming automobile industry. These conditions created heavy demands on the U.S. in Europe and Japan and also in third markets for fuels and industrial materials as well as for capital equipment for their production. One by one these shortages disappeared, and with them, the exceptional support which they had provided to U.S. exports.[3]

It might be added that it was relatively easy for the Europeans and the Japanese to catch up with new production techniques developed in the mature steel industry. The U.S. lead in the other, less mature industries was apparently maintained, and the U.S. managed to increase their exports throughout the period under review, despite the apparent decline of the country's overall competitive position.

A somewhat different explanation for the U.S. international trade position was suggested by R. Vernon who hypothesized that:

---

[1] Ibid., pp. 30–32.
[2] The one exception is provided by pharmaceuticals, a group made up of products belonging to all phases of the product cycle. It may well be that close examination of the items listed amongst pharmaceutical exports will reveal most of them to be 'mature' drugs.
[3] Ibid., p. 52.

Given the relatively high cost of labor and the plentiful supply of capital, there is a strong drive among U.S. producers constantly to be scanning the possibilites of designing products which would represent the substitution of capital for labor. This pressure has led to the early design of such direct labor saving devices as heavy fork-lift trucks and jumbo earth-moving equipment, and of such indirect labor-saving devices as dirt-resistant and weather-resistant building materials and drip-dry fabrics.[1]

These products, according to Vernon, begin to enter world trade as '. . . some prospective users of labor-saving products abroad [who], according to the calculus of capital budgetry, find it economic to buy such devices before they are generally needed in the economy'.[2] The market for labour-saving imports continues to grow as labour costs abroad rise and capital becomes more abundant. Eventually foreign markets grow to such an extent that large-scale local production becomes profitable, and the U.S. export dominance declines. 'Indeed', concludes Vernon, 'at this point, producers operating in areas with labor costs below those of the U.S. have displaced the U.S. product to some extent in third country markets and even in the U.S. itself . . .'.

Vernon's views coincide essentially with those of Burenstam-Linder. Both suggest that internal demand determines the characteristics of a country's exports. On the other hand, the product-cycle approach puts the emphasis on the technical capabilities of the supplier as the major determinant of trade flows. The two views do not necessarily conflict, however; by the time an importing country is ready to establish an import-replacing industry in its own economy, the product is likely to have passed from the early to more mature stages of the cycle.

At this juncture it might be useful to modify somewhat the product-cycle approach. The reader might object to the labelling of consumer appliances such as refrigerators as mature products while referring to electrical generators as second-phase products. In the first place, generators preceded refrigerators chronologically. In the second place, it is quite likely that refrigerators, with their frequent model changes, undergo more extensive modifications in design than generators.

The chronological argument is of little relevance, since it was

---

[1] R. Vernon, 'The Trade Expansion Act in Perspective', in W. S. Decker (ed.), *Emerging Concepts in Marketing, Proceedings of the Winter Conference of the American Marketing Association* (December 1962), p. 384.
[2] Ibid., p. 383.

not claimed that different products pass through phases of equal length. A diverse pattern is, as a matter of fact, likely to be the rule, since changes in technology, consumer habits, and capital requirements, which are some of the factors affecting the life-span of products, vary considerably between different industries and individual items. Thus ten years in the history of electronics products may cover a good part of the cycle whereas the same period of time may usher in few changes in steel.

The next factor to recognize is that not all products go through the whole cycle. Certain manufactures simply never reach the mass production stage because demand is too restricted. Ships, for example, are custom-made to very rigid specifications of the customers, who are unlikely to order many duplicates, even when the original model was entirely satisfactory. In cases such as these, the stability of the technology should be regarded as the decisive criterion for classifying the product. Shipbuilding technology is quite stable, and few changes of substance have been introduced in the construction methods during the last few decades. The industry is therefore classified here as mature.[1]

D. THE EARLY PHASE — AN OPPORTUNITY FOR SMALL DEVELOPED COUNTRIES

In contrast with the mature phase, the early stages in the product cycle are characterized by an unstable production function, which tends to be relatively labour-intensive. Specialized machinery is rarely used at this stage, since the small size of the market and the frequent changes in the design of the products and the production process do not justify heavy investments in inflexible equipment suitable for long runs. Multi-purpose machines which are relatively slow are used instead to facilitate flexibility and to minimize investment.

In order to gain a competitive advantage in new products manufacturers must, as was noted earlier, be in a position to obtain scientific and technical know-how at comparatively low costs. They must, in addition, have easy access to external economies represented by independent supply sources, ancillary services, and communication facilities. While the range of services supplies and

[1] Information on recent developments in the U.S. and the Japanese shipbuilding industries suggests that radically new construction methods are being adopted by enterprising shipyards in these countries. If close examination of these methods shows them to be considerably different from the existing ones, shipbuilding ought to be reclassified as a second-phase industry.

other external economies available to U.S. manufacturers is undoubtedly the largest in the world, other countries possess engineering and scientific talents which might be obtained at comparatively lower costs.

A word about the definition of the term 'scientific and engineering inputs' is in order at this juncture. It was stated earlier in connexion with the discussion of the Hecksher-Ohlin theorem and the 'Leontief Paradox' that the term 'labour input', when not properly defined, may easily mean different things in different countries. The average U.S. labourer possesses skills, mental habits, and knowledge dissimilar to those possessed by his Indian or Nigerian counterparts. Thus while an automatic lathe, if properly operated, will be capable of turning out screws of a certain size and tolerance regardless of its location, the same is not true of 'labour'. Consequently, one hour of labour in India cannot be compared to a unit similarly defined in the U.S. In order to be meaningful a comparison must specify in more detail the kind of labour, the skills required, or the job content.

Fortunately an unambiguous definition of scientific and engineering know-how is feasible. A scientist will be defined here as a person possessing an advanced degree in one of the sciences, and an engineer as one having an engineering degree. The term 'scientific and engineering inputs' will refer to the value of the services rendered by scientists and engineers as measured by their employment costs. This definition has the advantage of being universally applicable, since science and engineering degrees are awarded the world over for the attainment of professional and academic standards which are pretty well comparable. To the possible objection that the quality of academic education may vary considerably between countries, it might be retorted that the same is equally true about variations between different institutions within the same country. The definition obviously has its shortcomings, but it is adequate for the purpose at hand.

The above definition suggests that the average productivity of engineers and scientists tends to vary little from country to country. One would therefore expect an Israeli possessing a doctor's degree in chemical engineering to be on the average as efficient as his U.S. counterpart, provided that both worked under similar conditions.

The industrial leaders, headed by the U.S., are usually and rightfully regarded as possessing the managerial, manpower, and capital resources as well as the external economies which are necessary for the development of new products and for carrying them through the early phases of the cycle. The size of the U.S. market, its wealth, diversity, and complexity, provide, in turn, an environment which is conducive to the development of new products and their early introduction.

Smaller developed countries such as Switzerland, Holland, Sweden, and even Israel, which lack a comparable array of resources, need not necessarily limit their horizons to mature industries. They may have an advantage in certain new products.[1] New products have been shown here to be characterized by the intensive use of scientific and technical know-how on the one hand, and by the relative unimportance of the contribution of managerial talents and capital on the other. The subtle but nevertheless real difference between the nature of the early and accelerating phases of the product cycle suggests that smaller countries may possess a comparative advantage in certain categories of new products, provided they have at their disposal an adequate pool of comparatively inexpensive scientific and engineering know-how. The industrial leaders are likely to have a competitive edge in products whose development and manufacture involve extensive utilization of external economies, capital, and managerial inputs. The small developed economies in turn might possess a competitive potential in products less dependent on external economies and more dependent on extensive utilization of scientific and engineering inputs.

The problems involved in translating this potential into reality are discussed in detail in Chapters III and V. The preceding analysis is summarized in graphic form and recapitulated in a somewhat more rigorous fashion in the appendix of this chapter.

Appendix: Summary and Graphic Presentation

Figure 2 summarizes the analysis by illustrating how international competitiveness is affected by the interaction between the

---

[1] The countries classified here as small and developed are distinguished from the industrial leaders in several respects. (1) They have to import a high proportion of the goods and services consumed locally, because they lack many raw materials and natural resources. (2) Domestic markets for numerous products are too small to allow local industries to operate at an optimal scale unless they export a high proportion of their output. (3) External economies are comparatively limited.

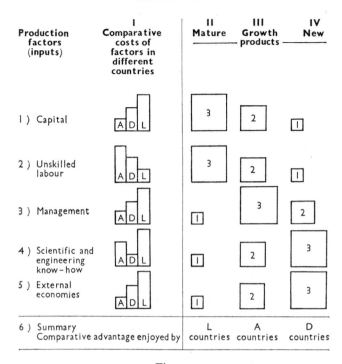

Figure 2
*The relationship between Factor Costs, International
Competitiveness, and Maturity of Products*

Footnote: The height of the rectangles in column I is not intended to suggest the
exact or even approximate relationship which exists between the cost of different
inputs in the three country groups; it merely ranks them. Similarly, the area of
the rectangles in columns II, III, and IV is intended merely to emphasize the
different factor intensities of the three product groups.

maturity of different product groups, the stages of industrial
development, and the relative prices of different manufacturing
inputs. Five inputs which affect production costs directly or indirectly are shown in the diagram; capital, unskilled labour, management, professional and scientific labour and external economies.
Materials and supplies were left out of the diagram because their
availability and cost do not necessarily vary systematically with
maturity, or with the state of industrial development. To the extent
that materials and supplies include fabricated parts or sub-
assemblies (rather than plain raw materials) obtained from sub-
contractors and other external suppliers, they are accounted for by
external economies.

The relative costs (or scarcity) of these inputs in three groups of countries denoted 'A', 'D', and 'L' are represented by the rectangles shown at the left-hand column. 'A' stands for the world's most advanced industrial economies, led by the United States. 'D' denotes the smaller developed economies, such as Holland, Switzerland, and Israel, which lack important raw materials and depend heavily on foreign trade. Less developed countries such as India, Hong Kong, and Turkey, where 'the initial stages of industrialization have been completed',[1] belong to the last group denoted by 'L'.

The rectangles shown in the left-hand column rank the different inputs by costs per unit of output. Efficiency as well as unit costs (or, more precisely, relative scarcity) were taken into consideration in determining these ranks.[2] A glance at the second row indicates, for example, that unskilled labour is assumed to be comparatively cheaper in the less developed countries than in the advanced economies. The cost of unskilled labour is shown, in turn, to be higher in the 'A' countries than in the 'D' countries. The diagram reflects the assumption that even though U.S. unskilled labourers may be more efficient than their Indian counterparts (when both are using identical equipment), U.S. wages per unit of output are on the average higher than in India. The relative costs of the remaining inputs in the different economies may be similarly gauged. The 'D' countries are shown to have a competitive edge in professional and scientific labour, while the industrial leaders' competitive position is strongest in three elements: management, external economies, and capital.

The input contents of 'typical' or 'representative' mature, growth, and new products are shown in columns II, III, and IV respectively. The area of the rectangles which are drawn opposite each production factor is indicative of the proportions in which these inputs are combined in the manufacture of the three product groups. Column II indicates that the inputs *most intensively* utilized in mature products are unskilled labour and capital. Professional labour and external economies, on the other hand,

---

[1] A. K. Cairncross, *Factors in Economic Development* (London, George Allen and Unwin Ltd., 1962), p. 206.

[2] In the present context efficiency should be viewed as a function of general education, working habits, and industrial experience. Professional training and capital equipment, whose important role in the enhancement of productivity is explicitly recognized in the diagram, are treated as separate inputs.

figure most prominently in new products, while growth products are shown to be the least specialized as far as production inputs are concerned.

Variations between the utilization of the different inputs in the manufacture of the three product groups are indicated by numbers shown at the centre of the rectangles. These numbers range from one to three; the more intensive the utilization of the input, the higher the number. It can be seen in the third row that management is considered to figure most importantly in growth products, less so in new ones, and least in mature products. Rows 4 and 5 show that the utilization of professional and scientific labour and of external economies varies inversely with maturity; the less mature the product the greater the relative importance of these inputs. Capital and unskilled labour, by contrast, are comparatively less important in new products and more important in mature ones, as is indicated by rows 1 and 2.

Optimal country/product combinations may be readily deduced from the figure. Each country will tend (in agreement with the Heckscher-Ohlin theorem) to have a comparative advantage in products containing a high proportion of inputs which are abundantly available to local industry, and a low proportion of inputs which are comparatively scarce. By analysing simultaneously the columns and rows of Figure 2 it is possible to determine the comparative advantage enjoyed by the different country groups.

The competitive position of the 'A' countries can be readily deduced from the figure. Examination of the left-hand column shows the relative cost of management, external economies, and capital to be lower in the 'A' countries than in the other country groups. One would therefore expect the 'A' countries to have a competitive edge in products containing a high proportion of these inputs. Column III shows that two of the production factors mentioned above—management and capital—figure more importantly in the manufacture of growth products than in either more mature or less mature ones. The comparative advantage of the 'A' countries may therefore be said to lie in growth products.

Next, the competitive position of the 'L' countries is examined. Column I indicates that the only input which is relatively less expensive in the 'L' countries than in the other economies is unskilled labour. This input is shown in column II to be more intensively utilized in the manufacture of mature products than in the less mature ones. This would suggest that the 'L' countries might be more competitive in mature products than in the other product groups. Further examination of column II tends to confirm the above observation. Mature products are shown to contain a low proportion of management, scientific and engineering labour, and external economies—all inputs which are comparatively scarce in the 'L' countries. Capital is the only expensive input to figure importantly in the manufacture of mature products.

Since no other product group contains a high proportion of unskilled labour, and, perhaps more important, since none contains such a low proportion of the inputs which are scarce in the 'L' countries, it may be concluded that these economies enjoy a comparative advantage in mature products. Their advantage, though, may be limited to products whose capital content is not too high.[1] Mature products which contain a very high proportion of capital may be produced at comparatively lower costs in the more advanced economies than in the 'L' countries.

Finally, the competitive position of the 'D' countries is considered. Column I shows scientific and engineering know-how to be the only production factor which is comparatively less expensive in the 'D' countries than in either of the other economies. These inputs are especially important in the manufacture of new products, as is indicated in column IV. Further examination of column IV reveals, however, that external economies, which are comparatively expensive in the 'D' countries, also figure importantly in new products. Since external economies are abundantly available in the 'A' countries, it may be concluded that both country groups are competitive in new products. The 'A' countries will have a competitive edge in new products containing a high proportion of external economies, whereas the 'D' countries will have the upper hand in products which are more dependent on inputs of professional and scientific labour.[2]

To summarize; the model presented here is, in a sense, an extension of the Heckscher-Ohlin model, which explains comparative advantage in terms of the relative costs of the inputs utilized in the manufacture of different products. Starting essen-

---

[1] The data presented in Chapter IV indicate that the substitution of capital for labour can proceed relatively far before the cost of capital begins to affect adversely the competitiveness of the less-developed countries.

[2] Chapter V contains a detailed example which illustrates the conditions that must be fulfilled for a 'D' country to be competitive in new products.

tially from the same premises, the present model postulates that factor intensities of different product groups, as well as their technical and market characteristics, vary with maturity in a systematic fashion.[1] As the products progress from the early phases of the product cycle to the more mature ones, the rate of input utilization changes in the manner indicated in Figure 2.

The reader should bear in mind that the model ranks the different inputs by their relative scarcity in the three country groups, and specifies the *direction* in which input utilization varies with maturity; it does not, and cannot, specify the *levels* of input utilization, which vary from product to product.

The 'L' countries, for example, tend, according to the model, to have a comparative advantage in mature products, since, when compared to growth or new products, mature products tend to contain a higher proportion of inputs which are abundant in the 'L' countries, and a lower proportion of scarce inputs. An examination of any particular mature product may show the level of scarce inputs to be higher than that of the abundant inputs. Since it is not the rate of input utilization but rather the level of the different inputs weighted by their relative cost which determines comparative production costs, the 'L' countries cannot be regarded as having a comparative advantage in *all* mature products. The same reasoning applies, of course, to the other product/country combinations.

The above suggests that the product-cycle model should be interpreted in a probabilistic sense. Assuming a random distribution of inputs among the universe of all products, one would expect the 'average' product or a large sample of products to have the characteristics suggested by the model. While the level of input utilization varies between industries and different products in a random fashion, the direction of input utilization changes systematically with maturity. Mature products will 'on the average' contain a higher proportion of unskilled labour and capital inputs and lower proportions of scientific and skilled labour inputs than new products.

Frequency distributions of products competitively manufactured by different country groups will indicate distinctive tendencies.

---

[1] The model also accepts the Heckscher-Ohlin assumption that the production function of manufactures varies little from country to country. See p. 10 for a detailed discussion of this assumption.

Industry in the less developed ('L' countries) will tend to concentrate its output in the more mature section of the maturity continuum, and output of the small developed ('D' countries) will tend to concentrate at the opposite end of the continuum. Industrial output of the industrial leaders ('A' countries) will be more broadly distributed and the mean of the distribution will be located somewhere in between those of the 'D' and the 'L' countries. The three frequency distributions are shown in Figure 3.

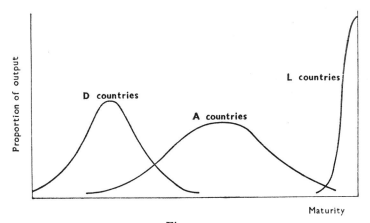

Figure 3
Output of Export and Import-Competing Industries in
the Three Country Groups—Frequency Distributions

The figure shows output of the 'D' countries and the 'A' countries to be normally distributed, whereas the distribution of the output of the 'L' countries is shown to be skewed to emphasize the concentration of these countries on the most mature industries.

It should be noted that the figure shows the distribution of the output of export and of import-competing industries only. It does not purport to show how the output of industries which are not affected by international competition is distributed. The output of industries which are shielded against international competition because of high transportation or marketing costs, high tariffs, quota restrictions, or other Government regulations is therefore not considered in Figure 3.

Finally, by focusing on changes in input utilization rather than on input levels, the model emphasizes the dynamic aspects of comparative advantage. It indicates that comparative advantage enjoyed by a particular type of economy, at a given point in time, is liable to disappear as the product in question enters a more mature phase of the cycle. On the other hand, countries which have a disadvantage in certain products, because of their high content of scarce inputs, may find, as the products become more mature, that they are capable of producing them on a competitive basis.[1]

International competitiveness has so far been considered only from the point of view of comparative production costs. In order to reach the consumers, or industrial users, it is not sufficient for goods to be just produced; they have to be marketed as well. In the following chapter the analysis focuses on the problems involved in marketing products across national borders.

---

[1] Several normative implications are suggested by the above. These will be discussed in Chapter IV.

III

INTERNATIONAL COMPETITIVENESS: THE MARKETING FUNCTION

A. IMPORT-REPLACING V. EXPORTING

It was noted in Chapter I that the ability to manufacture at competitive prices does not constitute a sufficient condition for exporting. A number of inhibiting factors act as deterrents to the realization of the latent competitive advantage which a country may possess. Consideration of the problems involved in exporting products to foreign countries may be helpful in identifying some of these 'trade-braking factors'[1] and understanding their nature.

This chapter discusses the view that local manufacturers enjoy as a rule important advantages over foreign competitors and that these advantages are not confined to barriers placed in the way of the foreign suppliers by Governments on the one hand (in the form of rules and regulations such as customs duties or quota restrictions) and by distance on the other.[2]

Some insight into the problems encountered by exporters may be gained by considering the difference between exporting and replacing imports. Both functions involve competition with foreign suppliers, and the ability to perform either points to the existence of competitive advantage. Yet only a naive observer would

---

[1] The term was coined by S. Burenstam-Linder.

[2] It might be noted in this connexion that whereas customs duties always confer an advantage on the local manufacturers, since they, by their very nature, penalize imports, the same is not necessarily true of transportation costs. There is first the obvious case of having the closest source of supply across the border rather than in one's country. Haulage charges from Detroit to Toronto are likely to be lower than from Detroit to San Francisco despite the fact that Detroit and San Franciso are both in the U.S. and Toronto is across the border, in Canada. Moreover, the cost differential between different methods of transportation compensates at times for longer distances. Ocean freight is cheaper than any existing method of land transportation when long distances are involved. This fact enabled Israeli firms, for example, to compete successfully on several occasions for large bids of cement shipments to the Florida coast, against U.S. manufacturers, whose plants were located much closer to the customer.

disregard the distinction between the nature of the tasks involved in displacing a foreign competitor in one's own market and successfully competing with him on his home ground.

Exporters must overcome more obstacles than the local manufacturer who tries to replace foreign suppliers. Some of these obstacles cannot be assigned a dollar value, but failure to consider them may lead to incorrect conclusions about the nature of the problems involved, and to the formulation of policies which fail to bring about the desired results. Analyses of export marketing problems which consider only transportation costs and trade policy issues cannot be meaningful to individual firms involved in the formulation of export policies. To such firms, customs duties and transportation costs represent exogenous data which must be taken into account, but which cannot be altered by the firm's actions. The problems which the exporter has to grapple with and *solve*, one way or the other, include: creating a viable information network; penetrating the foreign market and maintaining an acceptable market share; establishing of a foreign sales organization and keeping a minimum degree of control over such an organization.

None of these problems are absent in a domestic situation, especially where the firms in question serve regional or large national markets. Exporting, however, means that goods are shipped across the border and are marketed in foreign countries. These facts create a number of problems which the exporter finds more difficult to tackle than a domestic manufacturer. To start with, consider the problem of obtaining market information. Data concerning the size of the market for particular products, including the volume of shipments and even average prices, are usually available in the form of import statistics. Comparable information about domestically produced goods is not always obtainable so easily, owing to the difficulty involved in data collection and the reluctance of producers to divulge information.

Secondly, once local manufacturers decide to establish import-competing industries, they are often able to enlist the help of their foreign competitors and/or their local distributors, who might prefer to co-operate with the new enterprise rather than risk the displeasure of the Government, organized labour, and other organizations that stand to benefit from the establishment of indigenous industries. Through co-operation with former importers, the new enterprise may be able to gain access to the market through established channels of distribution which had previously handled imported goods.[1]

B. EXPORT V. DOMESTIC MARKETING PROBLEMS

Some of the difficulties involved in marketing manufactured products in foreign countries are illustrated in the following example, which is concerned with an export-oriented industrial project in Israel.

The Israel Government was approached in 1958 by a U.S. manufacturer of flat glass products who sought to transfer his manufacturing plant from the U.S. to Israel. He planned to continue to service his existing U.S. customers, who included firms such as Woolworth's, Kresge, and other chain stores. The Industrial Advisory Group, an office charged with the examination of foreign investment proposals, was asked by the Ministry of Commerce and Industry to look into the matter. The group prepared a

TABLE III(1)

Production Costs of a Glass Products Plant in the
U.S. and Israel (in U.S. $)

	(1) U.S.	(2) Israel	(3) $\frac{2}{1}$%
Raw materials	325,406	232,000	71
Salaries and wages	321,694	221,000	65
General and administrative	74,484	98,220	132
Total ex-factory costs	721,585	551,220	76
Shipping costs		40,000	
U.S. customs duties		136,800	
Cost of goods produced ex-U.S. factory or warehouse	721,585	728,020	101

Source: Industrial Advisory Group, Ministry of Commerce and Industry; *A Project for the Erection in Israel of a Factory to Produce Mirrors, Glass Trays, Snack Tables and other Flat Glass Products* (Jerusalem, Government Printing Office, October 1958).

[1] The threat of administrative interference with continued profitable importation of their product was instrumental in the decision of numerous U.S. (and other) firms to establish manufacturing subsidiaries in the countries to which they had previously exported. See for example L. Gordon and E. L. Grommers, *United States Manufacturing Investment in Brazil* (Division of Research, Graduate School of Business Administration, Harvard University, Boston), 1962, which describes in detail the methods used by the Brazilian Government to induce U.S. automotive producers to establish assembly plants in Brazil.

report which compared the production costs of identical products in the U.S. and Israel. Their figures are summarized in Table III(1).

The calculations show that ex-factory costs in Israel were expected to reach no more than 3/4 of the costs incurred in the U.S. The cost advantage of the proposed plant was of such magnitude that it was expected to be able to absorb shipping costs of $40,000 and steep customs duties exceeding 20 per cent. Total delivered costs, according to these calculations, were more or less equal in both countries.

The investor planned to keep his existing sales organization in the U.S. intact. Hence it was not necessary to compare the marketing costs of the existing and the proposed establishments. The investment proposal, as seen by the Industrial Advisory Group and the Israel Government, was very attractive. Few, if any, export products could be manufactured at such low costs at the then prevailing exchange rate in Israel. The project was eagerly accepted by the Government.

The Israeli cost advantage was manifested in several items: raw materials, consisting mainly of sheet glass, were less expensive in Israel than in the U.S.: additional savings were expected to be realized due to the proposed location of the plant. Proximity to a local glass factory and to the port of Haifa was going to save the firm considerable outlays on transportation and packaging. The biggest savings were expected in labour costs, which were estimated at only 65 per cent of the amount spent on salaries and wages in the U.S.

The cost advantage which Israel allegedly possessed in the manufacture of mirrors was not brought into being by the U.S. investor. He merely discovered this opportunity and proposed to exploit it. Why, it may be asked, were no mirrors exported from Israel previously? Could not an Israeli entrepreneur discover for himself that he might manufacture these items and sell them in the U.S. in competition with local producers?

The potential Israeli exporter suffered from a distinct disadvantage *vis-à-vis* his U.S. competitors; he lacked market information. Though experience showed that the U.S. market could indeed be profitably entered and served from Israel, the Israeli exporter could not learn about this opportunity without investing resources in market research in the U.S. In view of the knowledge subsequently gained, such an investment might indeed have been justified; but this could not have been ascertained by an outsider in advance. Moreover, as far as he was concerned, his limited funds might have been invested with equal probability of success in Britain, France, or Brazil.

The entry problems facing the exporter are not limited to the acquisition of market information. Resources have to be invested in developing a local marketing organization, establishing reliable channels of communication, and informing the customers of the availability of competitive imports. Suitable distributors have to be located and negotiated with, and arrangements for shipping and warehousing the products have to be made. Each of these factors may offset the manufacturing cost advantage which the exporter has, and none of them can be estimated with a high degree of certainty in advance without some face-to-face negotiations and intimate knowledge of the market.

The U.S. investor was in a much better position to assess his chances of succeeding in locating cheaper sources of supply and enhancing his competitive position. Easily available indicators such as average labour rates, power costs, &c. could suggest to him that production costs in Israel were cheaper than in the U.S.[1] His established contacts with U.S. customers and channels of distribution, and his knowledge of conditions obtaining in the market, gave him advantages which a potential Israeli competitor could not possibly share.

Having served the U.S. market for years, the American manufacturer benefited from knowledge of his customers' requirements and tastes. This knowledge could readily be translated into product specifications. The Israeli competitor would again have to spend effort and money in order to ascertain what it is that the American market requires. In a country such as the U.S. where the customer usually has a wide choice, knowledge of that kind is extremely important, and may spell the difference between success and utter failure.

The discussion in this section points to the existence of serious problems which handicap the marketing of goods across national boundaries. These difficulties have been largely neglected in the economic literature, which tends to emphasize comparative costs

---

[1] Admittedly, production costs could be cheaper still in Nigeria or in Turkey, but as long as any savings can be realized by locating the manufacturing operations abroad, the investor is better off than previously.

and national trade policies as the factors that determine the flow and composition of international trade. Government officials, economists, and businessmen who are concerned with the problems of expanding exports have come, however, to appreciate the decisive effect which the marketing function has on exports. A recent survey of more than 400 leading British exporters confirms this assertion, stating that

...Two thirds of the firms that had increased exports attributed their success to fresh efforts of some kind on the sales side. Only 19 per cent attributed success to any kind of improvement on the production side, and only 15 per cent to the increased attraction of overseas markets relative to the home market....There can be no doubting the implication that energetic and efficient selling is a key factor in increasing exports. Our export performance may depend in the long run on general remedies to make British industry more efficient, but in the short term it turns at least as much on specific measures to make selling efforts more effective...[1]

The argument thus far implies that the export potential of an industry or country may be less than fully realized, owing to marketing problems. It may be expected, by the same token, that when marketing problems are comparatively minor, export-oriented industries, whose comparative advantage is far from obvious, can be brought into being. A case in point is Israel's diamond industry. The fast growth rate which the industry achieved is demonstrated in Table III(2), which shows Israel's exports of non-industrial diamonds in the 1950–63 period.

TABLE III(2)

*Israel's Exports of Non-Industrial Diamonds
in Selected Years 1950–63*

Year	Export of Polished Diamonds *Carats '000*	*U.S. $'000*	Value Index *1950=100*
1950	119	8,810	100
1955	230	20,615	234
1958	330	32,959	374
1960	574	56,318	638
1961	669	65,284	740
1962	838	82,339	934
1963	1,047	104,017	1,135

Source: Ministry of Commerce and Industry, *Program for Israel's Industrial Development, Second outlook 1965-70* (Jerusalem, GPO 1964), p. 377.

[1] Political and Economic Planning, 'Firms and their Exports', *Planning* (London, vol. XXX, No. 483, 8 November 1964), p. 286.

The performance of the industry cannot possibly be explained within the framework of traditional comparative advantage theories, since all the ingredients of comparative advantage are missing in Israel. No diamond mines are located in the country, and the industry is obliged to import all raw materials from Africa (a fact which reduces the value added of diamonds to less than 30 per cent of the sales price). Neither is there any reason to assume that the labour force is peculiarly suited for the job of polishing. Diamond polishers are mostly new immigrants who were trained in their profession *after* their arrival in the country. Most had no previous connexion of any sort with the industry. Moreover, local demand for diamonds is practically non-existent, and the bulk of the industry's output is exported. Yet by 1963 Israel had become one of the largest diamond polishers in the world, employing 8,000 workers who accounted for 28 per cent of the world's employment in diamond cutting and polishing.

The remarkable performance of the industry can be explained by its management's origin and its marketing methods. The industry was founded in the thirties by immigrants from the Low Countries (which were then, and are now, important diamond centres). These people possessed management experience and professional know-how which they successfully applied in their new environment. More important, they brought with them a good deal of market knowledge and trade connexions, which they were able to exploit to great advantage after the war when diamond trading was revived.

The highly organized nature of the selling function enabled the exporters to dispose of their output with ease, offering it in the specialized exchanges or bourses located in London, Brussels, or New York. The demand from the point of view of the individual producer is infinitely elastic. Any quantity which he can produce will be sold at prices established with the aid of objective criteria which he understands and accepts. Moreover, these criteria are universal and vary little from country to country. The sale of diamonds consequently requires only a minimum of marketing effort, and is not materially affected by the location of the manufacturer and his distance from the market.[1]

The examples discussed in this section suggest that the nature

---

[1] Air transport is used to convey diamonds, whose unit value in relation to weight is, of course, extremely high.

of the marketing function has a decisive influence on the exportability of different products, and that the marketing problems encountered by exporters vary from product to product. The following section examines the view that the product-cycle approach, which seeks to correlate the maturity of different products with some of their technological and market characteristics, may be useful in analysing the marketing aspects of international competitiveness.

C. THE PRODUCT-CYCLE MODEL AND THE EXPORT MARKETING FUNCTION

Chapter II showed how the rate of input utilization varies with the maturity of products and of industries. Changes in the structure of the supply of products obviously induce corresponding changes in the demand structure. These changes in turn have important implications for the choice of channels of distribution, of pricing and advertising policies, and of other components of the marketing function. Those aspects of the marketing function which are most relevant to the movements of goods across national borders are examined in some detail in this section.

Starting with the mature products, one might note several characteristics which make their export relatively easy. Specifications for these products and their prices are easily available, as was noted in Chapter II, and are easily communicated between manufacturers and customers. These characteristics make for a high degree of price elasticity. A supplier, whether he is a local manufacturer or a foreign exporter, has a distinct advantage over competitors if he can offer the product at a lower price. Regardless of whether the market is supplied by a multitude of small firms or whether a few oligopolists share it between them, ability to meet the price of the lowest seller determines the feasibility of entry.

Suppliers of agricultural commodities, industrial raw materials, and standardized non-differentiated manufactures will therefore find it relatively easy to engage in international trade once they adapt their products to the standards which are generally applicable in the markets they seek to enter. A piece of cotton cloth, for example, can be ordered anywhere in the world by specifying its contents in terms of fibre, type of weave, number of counts, &c. These specifications are universally understood; they mean exactly the same thing in any country. A manufacturer who can deliver cloth answering to this or that kind of description at competitive prices has a decisive edge over more expensive suppliers. And if he can, in addition, meet required delivery dates and have an acceptable reject rate, his chances of selling his product in competition with other local manufacturers may be rated as pretty high.

Many iron and steel products may, like textiles, be classified as near commodities. Demand for various kinds of steel having different shapes and sizes, is expressed in standard terms which are understood the world over. When the U.S. steel strike in 1959 shut down sources of local supply, the European steel industry had little difficulty in complying with requests for large quantities of steel to be delivered to the U.S. at relatively short notice.

This is not to say that exporters are competing on an equal footing with their local rivals—far from it. The exporters will probably have a harder job convincing local wholesalers that he can satisfy their requirements and service his accounts as satisfactorily as his more conveniently located competitors. Where the local manufacturer uses the services of a sales representative, the exporter will have to engage a stocking representative, whose commission is naturally higher than that of the former.[1] A broker will be needed to clear the imports through customs; commissions will be payable for special banking services—the opening of letters of credit, the transfer of funds, and their conversion into the exporter's currency. These expenses are payable by the exporter alone, and while they need not amount to a high percentage of the sales price, they do raise his marketing costs above those of his local competitor.

Information is not a free good, it must be paid for. Even when it is available the necessary knowledge will not get to the exporter on its own. He has to establish a mechanism by which he can acquire it. The characteristics of mature products and of their markets simplify the job of getting the necessary information, but do not obviate it. Consequently, it is not sufficient even for a textile or steel manufacturer to have a marginal cost advantage in manufacturing. The advantage must be large enough to compensate for the extra marketing costs which he is certain to incur.

It may be concluded that the more standardized the product

---

[1] A sales representative merely takes orders, which he passes on to the manufacturer. A stocking representative maintains stocks of the products he sells.

and the closer its resemblance to a commodity, the easier is the exporter's task of penetrating the foreign market and of maintaining his position there. By contrast, one would expect the exporter's job to become progressively more difficult, in the absolute sense and in comparison with local competition, as the products which he handles become less standardized.

To start with, standards of performance, of measurement, and of safety regulations vary from country to country. Failure to meet any of these standards excludes the supplier from the market regardless of the inherent quality of his product. Consider, for example, a machine tool manufacturer who seeks to sell his products abroad. His calibrating equipment must be denoted in centimetres if he desires to sell on the European continent and in inches if his market is the U.K. or the U.S. The electrical motor must be adapted to direct current in one country and to alternating current in a different location; the voltage must be adjusted; the same goes for the electrical contacts, the insulation, &c.

Two aspects of the exporter's marketing job, communication and servicing, acquire special significance with new products. It is obviously more difficult to communicate about non-standard products than about standard ones. It is more difficult for the supplier to inform the user about the product, as it is for the latter to determine whether the supplier can really satisfy his requirements. Occasionally moreover, changes in specifications are desirable, but since these are not stated clearly in standard terms, only face-to-face communications can establish this fact.

Servicing is more than a matter of routine check-up, minor adjustments, and replacement of faulty parts (in the case of industrial products). It becomes a very essential function which will determine whether a piece of equipment or component will be used by the buyer or not. Moreover, it is often necessary for the original equipment manufacturer to undertake the servicing himself, since no outside organization has the competence and experience to perform the job adequately. These problems will be discussed more fully in Chapter V, where the export problems of new products will be explored in detail. At present, it is sufficient to note on the basis of the examples discussed above that the exporter cannot adequately perform the same service function as a local manufacturer without incurring considerably higher costs than the former.

D. MARKETING COSTS AND ECONOMIES OF SCALE

The inclusion of marketing costs in the calculus of competitive advantage calls for a fresh look at the concept of economies of scale and for reconsidering their effect on the international competitiveness of different industries.

Industries supplying large markets are said to have an advantage over those which supply small markets because the former can benefit from economies of scale. Access to a large market enables firms to install special-purpose equipment, take advantage of bulk purchases, spread overhead and other fixed costs over a large number of units, and economize on the use of transport so as to minimize unit manufacturing costs. Ready access to large markets is said to help U.S. industry, for example, to keep unit manufacturing costs down to a level which enables it to compete in world markets even though U.S. wages are by far the highest in the world.

This reasoning is, however, fallacious once international trade is admitted into the economic model. If each national industry were to regard the world as the relevant market for its output, the scale of its manufacturing facilities need not be determined by the size of the domestic market. Thus, while the U.S. domestic appliances market may be several times the size of Britain's, British manufacturers need not plan their capacity on a smaller scale than their U.S. competitors, since both are competing for the same customers. In reality few manufacturers appear to regard the world market, or even that portion of the world market which is politically and economically accessible, as the relevant market for their products. Their horizons seem to encompass mainly the national market, and exports are treated at best as a marginal activity.[1]

The existence of transportation costs, customs duties, and other Government-imposed trade restrictions will undoubtedly restrict the scope of exports. The size of the export market will be further limited because of the difference between export and domestic marketing costs. The magnitude of the cost disadvantage of the exporter varies inversely, according to the product-cycle approach, with the maturity of the product; when a product is passing through

[1] See, for example, Kindleberger, *Foreign Trade and the National Economy.* The writer shows that of 46 countries surveyed by him, foreign trade (average of exports and imports of merchandise) exceeded 25 per cent of national income only in 15 cases, p. 10, Table 2-1.

the early phase of the cycle, the exporter's manufacturing cost advantage must be substantial in order to compensate for the large marketing cost differential from which the domestic manufacturer benefits.

If differential marketing costs are so high as to prevent manufacturers from gaining access to foreign markets, their output will be restricted to the domestic market, and if the domestic market is comparatively small, they will be deprived of the benefits of economies of scale which are available to those of their foreign competitors whose domestic market is large. Thus a situation may arise where a potential low-cost producer may be unable to compete internationally, *and even in his own market*, with a high-cost producer because export marketing costs exceed domestic marketing costs. The conditions under which this situation might arise are illustrated in the following example.

Consider two countries, A and B, where the following cost and market conditions exist for the output of a given industry.

	Country A	Country B
(1) Fixed costs[1]	200	200
(2) Unit variable costs	10	8
(3) Domestic marketing costs	3	3
(4) Export marketing costs	6	6

Additional Assumptions

(1) The size of the domestic market in country A is 90 units and in country B 10 units. The size of the markets is fixed over a wide price range.[2]

(2) Customers prefer to buy from a cheaper source regardless of whether the product is produced locally or is imported.

(3) Prices equal average costs unless otherwise stated.

(4) No customs duties and no quantitative trade restrictions are imposed.

(5) Both domestic and export marketing costs include transportation costs.

---

[1] For the sake of simplicity costs in both countries are expressed in identical monetary units.

[2] i.e. price elasticity is equal to zero over a wide price range.

A comparison of the cost structure of both countries will show country B to be the low-cost producer. If B were to produce for both markets, production costs would be $200 + 8 \times 100 = 1,000$; average unit costs would be 10. If A were to produce for both markets, production costs would be $200 + 10 \times 100 = 1,200$. Average unit costs would be 12.

If marketing costs are added to production costs the following competitive price structure will emerge:

	Country A	Country B
Domestic price	$12 + 3 = 15$	$10 + 3 = 13$
Export price	$12 + 6 = 18$	$10 + 6 = 16$

Country B is clearly the more competitive of the two. Both domestic and export prices are lower than those of country A. Yet, despite its cost advantage, B cannot compete with A in A's domestic market. Because of B's high marketing costs A's producers can offer their output in their domestic market at 15 whereas B's price will be 16.

This fact may affect the entire competitive posture of both countries. If B's producers are denied access to A's market owing to their higher prices, and if they must as a result confine themselves to their domestic market, their entire cost structure changes. Average unit production costs in B rise from 10 (if 100 units are produced) to 28 (if only 10 units are produced). Since A can export to B at the price of 18, B's producers will lose the domestic market.

To stay in business, producers in B may attempt to price their exports on a marginal cost basis. By charging 14 for their export, they could cover variable costs and undercut their competitors in A by 1. However, to remain in business in the long run, B's producers would have to recover fixed costs. If they were to attempt to make their domestic customers to bear this burden, the latter would have to pay 28 per unit. A's exporters would, under these conditions, have no difficulty in capturing B's market, and B's manufacturers would be unable to recover fixed costs. Moreover, to compete with cheap imports from B, A's manufacturers will be able, in the short run, to reduce their prices to 13. At this price, which is lower than that of B's imports, they can still recover variable costs. Hence, even in the short run B cannot compete with A in the latter's domestic market. Thus A will end up controlling both markets even though it is a high-cost producer.

The advantage of A cannot be explained by the large size of the country's domestic market alone. A's producers also benefit from protection afforded them by the existence of high export marketing costs. These high costs combine with the size of the market to maintain the competitive position of A's industry in the markets of both A and B. A more general model of the relationship between export marketing costs and economies of scale is developed in the Appendix of this chapter.

E. THE PRODUCT-CYCLE APPROACH —
RESTATEMENT AND SUMMARY

The main points of this chapter are summarized in Figure 4, which shows how comparative marketing costs of domestic and foreign suppliers, or, to be more precise, their non-production costs, compare over the various phases of the cycle.

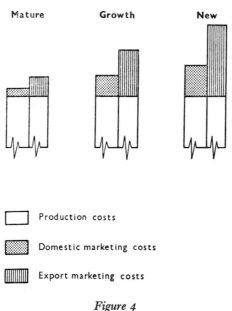

Figure 4
Domestic and Export Marketing Costs
Type of Products

Export marketing costs are shown to exceed marketing outlays of domestic competitors regardless of whether the products belong to the early, growth, or mature phases of the cycle. Relative differences between domestic and export marketing costs are largest when the products emerge from the research and development stage, and gradually decrease as the products become more mature. The differential never disappears completely, however, since the local manufacturer always has some cost advantage over the foreign exporter, if only because the latter's products have to be more securely packaged, his channels of distribution have to maintain a larger inventory, and the banker's services he requires are more extensive and, needless to say, more expensive. This cost differential is illustrated by the disparity between the height of the quadrangles, which increases from left to right. The height of the quadrangles similarly rises from left to right to indicate that the ratio of marketing to total costs tends to rise inversely with maturity.

The last statement has to be somewhat qualified to take into account those cases where advertising costs and other marketing outlays are deliberately boosted in order to differentiate between mature products having similar or almost identical physical and chemical properties. Cigarettes, coffee, gasoline, detergents, and numerous other household goods figure prominently among such products.

Conceptually, this objection might be taken care of by distinguishing between those parts of the marketing function which *must* be performed by the manufacturer, and those which *can* be taken care of by the wholesalers and retailers. The fortunes of individual U.S. coffee companies may be radically affected by the success of their advertising strategy. This fact, however, is unlikely to affect either the prices at which Colombian coffee planters can dispose of their crop in the U.S. or the method used by wholesalers to buy the coffee. Coffee growers may decide to integrate forward, and enter the U.S. coffee marketing business. Their roles as marketers and exporters have, however, no necessary bearing on each other.

The marketing of less mature products, by contrast, cannot be so readily divorced from their manufacture. Cars, machine tools, and electrical generators, for example, cannot be sold without providing the buyer with a minimum of post-sale services and spare parts. Some of these (such as provision of spare parts and service manuals) must be provided by the manufacturer to the distributor or agent, even when the latter operates an independent business in which the manufacturer has no proprietary stake. It may be concluded, therefore, that while the marketing costs of certain mature products do not conform to the pattern suggested by Figure 4, this fact has no bearing on the problems of *foreign entry*, which the figure is intended to illustrate.

The fact that export marketing is more expensive than domestic marketing tends to affect the range of product which can be marketed abroad. Like transportation costs and import duties, differential marketing costs strengthen the competitive position of the local manufacturer *vis-à-vis* foreign competition. This factor, however, influences different industries in varying degrees. Figure 4 shows that domestic manufacturers of second-phase products are relatively more immune to foreign competition than the producers of more mature products. Goods belonging to the first phase of the product cycle enjoy, in turn, a higher degree of protection than those belonging to the second phase. The figure also suggests that different countries are likely to be affected in varying degrees by the gap between export and domestic marketing costs.

Exports from the 'D' countries will be most adversely affected, since, as was shown in Chapter II, these countries have a comparative advantage in new products. Domestic manufacturers of these products were shown to enjoy considerable protection against foreign competition. The marginal nature of the advantage enjoyed by the 'D' countries in new products was demonstrated in Chapter II. It was attributed to the dependence of new product manufacturing on external economies, which are comparatively expensive in the 'D' countries. The marketing cost advantage of the foreign manufacturers of new products will tend to limit further the range of new products which the 'D' countries can expect to manufacture, on a competitive basis, for the export markets.

Exporters located in the 'A' countries will be penalized to a lesser degree by the differential between export and domestic marketing costs. These countries were shown in Chapter II to have a comparative advantage in growth products. The marketing cost advantage enjoyed by domestic manufacturers of these products is comparatively smaller than in the case of new products. Moreover, the competitive strength of the 'A' countries in growth products is based on the capital intensity of these products, and on their high content of managerial talents. Both these inputs were shown to be comparatively cheaper in the 'A' countries than in the other countries. Consequently, domestic producers of growth products in the 'L' and 'D' countries are unlikely to receive significant protection from the higher marketing costs of the 'A' countries' exporters.

The 'L' countries will be least affected by the differential between export and domestic marketing costs. These countries' comparative advantage lies in mature products. The difference between export and domestic marketing costs of mature products is comparatively small, and the protection enjoyed by the domestic manufacturers against foreign competitors in their home markets is therefore rather limited.

In summary, the analytical framework presented here suggests that the international competitiveness of different economies depends on the relative scarcity of production factors on the one hand, and on the complexity of the manufacturing and marketing functions on the other. The last two factors vary in turn in a systematic fashion with the maturity of the products under consideration.

Abundantly endowed with managerial talents, capital, skills, and external economies, the industrial leaders enjoy a comparative advantage in growth (second-phase) products, which can be competitively manufactured only when all these inputs are in abundant supply.

Scientific and engineering skills are comparatively cheap in smaller developed economies, which have limited natural resources and external economies. These countries may develop competitive strength in new (first-phase) products which contain a high proportion of skill and science inputs, provided that their manufacture does not depend on intensive utilization of external economies.

Less developed economies can exploit their ample supply of unskilled labour most advantageously by the manufacture of mature (third-phase) products. While the production process is frequently capital-intensive, technology and equipment can be easily imported, and, equally significant, scarce production factors such as management and scientific know-how are of comparatively little importance.

Marketing costs too affect international competitiveness. Exporters incur, as a rule, higher marketing costs than their domestic competitors, since foreign sales involve higher transportation and financial charges, customs duties, more complicated selling arrangements, larger inventories, &c. The cost and complexity of two factors in particular, communications and servicing, are significantly affected. They increase directly with distance and inversely with maturity. The ensuing cost differential, which is beneficial to local manufacturers, tends to encourage the establishment of import-replacing industries while retarding the development of export-oriented enterprises.

This concludes the first part of the study, in which the product-cycle model of international competitiveness has been outlined. Some aspects of this model are tested in the following chapter on empirical data pertaining to the characteristics and international performance of the U.S. electronics industry.

Appendix: The Relationship Between the Relative Size of Markets, Export and Domestic Marketing Costs, and International Competitiveness

Assume two countries A and B where the production and marketing conditions for a given product are as follows:

	Country A	Country B
Fixed costs	F	F
Unit variable costs	Pa	Pb
Domestic marketing costs	M	M
Export marketing costs	X	X
Size of the domestic market (in units)	a	b

To simplify the analysis, it is assumed that fixed production costs, unit domestic marketing costs, and export marketing costs are equal in both countries.[1] The only inequalities are:

(1) $$Pa > Pb$$

(2) $$X > M$$

---

[1] For other assumptions regarding pricing policies, demand elasticity, &c. see p. 53.

i.e. unit variable production costs are higher in A than in B and export marketing costs exceed domestic marketing costs. Despite the fact that A's production costs are higher than B's, the latter's competitive position in the former's market is by no means assured. The condition for foreign entry is

$$(3) \qquad \frac{F}{a+b} + Pb + X < \frac{F}{a} + Pa + M$$

Four elements contribute towards the long-run competitive position of the two trading countries: production costs (including both fixed and variable), marketing costs, relative market share, and the absolute level of the fixed costs. The conditions regarding market shares and the level of fixed costs require some elaboration.

The condition of B's entry into A may be restated as follows:

$$(4) \qquad Pa - Pb > X - M + \frac{F}{a+b} - \frac{F}{a}$$

If B has no domestic market at all, then $\frac{F}{a+b} - \frac{F}{a} = 0$ and the condition for B's entry becomes $Pa - Pb > X - M$.

If B has a domestic market, its production cost advantage need not be quite as large since, for a positive b, $\frac{F}{a+b} - \frac{F}{a} < 0$.

If for example $b = a$, then the condition for entry becomes

$$(5) \qquad Pa - Pb > X - M - \frac{F}{a}$$

In general, the larger b in relation to a, the smaller the production cost advantage B needs to enter A.

The level of the fixed costs F also affects the condition of entry. If $F = 0$ market shares cease to affect average costs and the condition of entry again becomes $Pa - Pb > X - M$. The higher the level of F, the more weight is exerted by relative market shares. If F is very high and A's domestic market is considerably larger than B's, then A could gain entry into B despite the fact that its production costs exceed those of B. For this condition to materialize it is necessary that

$$(6) \qquad \frac{F}{a+b}+Pa+X<\frac{F}{b}+Pb+M$$

i.e.

$$(7) \qquad \frac{F}{b}-\frac{F}{a+b}>Pa-Pb+X-M$$

IV

AN EMPIRICAL TEST OF THE PRODUCT-CYCLE MODEL: THE UNITED STATES ELECTRONICS INDUSTRY

A. INTRODUCTION

A MODEL of international competitiveness has been outlined in the first part of this study. The model is based on the proposition that the relative maturity of the industry in which different countries possess competitive strength is negatively correlated with the stage of economic development reached by them; the more developed the economy, the greater the advantage which it has in growth products. The ability of the product-cycle model to explain the competitive strength which a particular country possesses in a given industry is tested in the present chapter on empirical data pertaining to the U.S. electronics industry.

Several economic and technological attributes possessed by the electronics industry make it especially interesting for the purpose at hand. To start with, the industry is extremely diverse. It manufactures a large variety of products, ranging from radios, which have been produced in the U.S. for several decades, through electronic computers, scarcely known before 1950, to lasers, devices developed in recent years having a tremendous potential in the fields of communication, medicine and energy transmission which have yet to make their commercial impact. Electronic goods may therefore be found in all phases of the product cycle throughout the whole spectrum of maturity. At the same time electronic products share certain technological characteristics: their manufacture involves the assembly of a number of basic components which are common to a large variety of products. Thus transistors are incorporated in both radios and computers, and vacuum tubes having basically similar characteristics form the core of television sets and radar instruments alike.

Moreover, the line between electronic and non-electronic products is commonly drawn on the basis of technology. Electronics

utilise in practical applications the principles of the physical sciences which pertain to the direction and control of electricity in a gas, vacuum, liquid or solid state material... Electronic products are distinguished from purely electrical articles by the fact that whereas electricity flows through the circuits of both, the electron tubes and semi-conductors in the electronic products discharge, direct, control, or otherwise influence the flow of electricity.[1]

This definition accords with that of the product-cycle model, which uses technological criteria to distinguish between different product groups.[2] Since the U.S. Bureau of the Census classifies electronic products on the basis of the above definition, it is possible to use the industry data without having to make allowances for subgroups and product lines which do not 'belong' within the framework of the above definition.[3]

Another characteristic of the U.S. electronics industry makes it useful for the purpose at hand. The volume of international trade in electronics is considerable, and competition in the world markets appears to be keen. The U.S., moreover, is a major trader in electronic products; its imports and exports constitute a significant proportion of world trade.[4] If trade in electronics were insignificant, random factors might have been responsible for wide variations in the imports and exports of different countries. Since trade, however, is considerable, it is legitimate to attribute major changes in the international performance of the U.S. industry and its foreign rivals to their respective competitive strength.

The model postulates, it will be recalled, that the more developed an economy the greater the advantage it possesses in growth products and the lesser its advantage in mature ones. If this postulate is to be accepted, it must be shown that the competitive position of the U.S., the world's foremost industrial leader, is

---

[1] Electronics Industry Association: Before the U.S. Tariff Commission and the Trade Information Committee, *Views of the U.S. Electronics Industry* (Washington, March 1964). This publication contains a wealth of data organized and presented on a systematic and consistent basis. It will be extensively quoted throughout the chapter. Future quotes will be denoted *Views*.

[2] See Kuznets's definition of new products on page 17.

[3] The above does not imply that all products manufactured by the industry are classified on a basis which is suitable for testing the model. This point will be further elaborated upon in the following section.

[4] *Views*, Table XXI.

strongest in comparatively new electronic products, while being relatively weak in the more mature ones.

In order to test the proposition it is first necessary to devise criteria for the identification and measurement of 'comparative maturity' and 'competitive strength'. Terms such as these may have different meanings in different circumstances, and the criteria by which they are judged may vary from case to case. These methodological matters will be considered one at a time as the examination of the empirical data proceeds. The analysis proper is preceded by a description of the industry's principal sectors and their major product lines, and by a brief note on the nature of the data presented in this chapter.

B. THE INDUSTRY AND ITS MAJOR PRODUCT LINES

The U.S. electronics industry is commonly divided into the following six sectors, which between them account for about 80 per cent of the industry's output. (1) Government and industrial electronics—S.I.C.[1] 3662; (2) special-purpose electron tubes—S.I.C. 3673; (3) components and accessories—S.I.C. 3679; (4) consumer products—S.I.C. 3651; (5) radio and T.V. receiving tubes—S.I.C. 3671; (6) cathode ray picture tubes—S.I.C. 3672.

Two of the groups, Government and industrial electronics and consumer products, manufacture for final users—industry, Government, and consumers. The remaining four groups are engaged primarily in the manufacture of components used by the former sectors. The major products of each sector are listed in Table IV(1).

Three sectors (special-purpose electron tubes, radio and T.V. receiving tubes, and cathode ray picture tubes) manufacture the traditional components of the industry—electron tubes. The consumer products sector is the major customer for receiving tubes and cathode ray (TV) tubes, whereas special-purpose tubes such as transmitting, klystron, and microwave tubes are used chiefly by the industrial and military electronics sector. While the products of the three tube-manufacturing sectors have many technical similarities, the end use, and the techniques involved in their

---

[1] S.I.C.=Standard Industrial Classification, as used by the U.S. Bureau of the Census.

TABLE IV(1)

E.S. Electronics Industry: Principal Sectors and Products

Component Sectors

S.I.C. Number Sector Title	3671 Receiving Tubes	3672 Cathode Ray Tubes	3679 Components and Accessories	3673 Special Purpose Tubes
Major Product Groups	radio receiving tubes T.V. receiving tubes	T.V. cathode ray tubes	solid state devices inductors transformers capacitors resistors, &c.	transmitting tubes industrial tubes special purpose tubes

Finished Products Sectors

S.I.C. Number Sector Title	3651 Consumer Products	3662 Government and Industrial Products
Major Product Groups	radio receivers T.V. receivers musical apparatus	radio and T.V. broadcasting equipment communication equipment field detection apparatus

Source: *Views*, pp. 10, 11.

manufacture, are sufficiently different to explain their separate classification by the Bureau of the Census.

Transistors, capacitors, micro-circuits, and other semiconducting devices are manufactured by the components and accessories sector, which supplies the Government, industrial, and the consumer products markets. In the case of the latter, solid state components have displaced vacuum tubes in numerous applications and have facilitated the introduction of several products such as transistor radios and transistorized tape-recorders. The development of a large and growing number of communication, control, and computation techniques and equipment has been facilitated by the availability of small and reliable semiconducting devices, whose origin can be traced to the invention of the transistor in 1948.

Figures pertaining to the six sectors discussed above provide the basis for the analysis. However, census industrial classifications are not at all times best suited for the purpose at hand. The product-cycle model distinguishes between different products by the degree of their maturity[1] and seeks to explain competitiveness in terms of this criterion. Ideally, therefore, all products grouped within a particular sector should be equally mature. One can hardly expect the Census Bureau to have used the maturity criterion (however defined) as a basis for classification. Colour television, for example, is grouped together with radio and monochrome television in one sector. While colour television can be shown to belong to the growth phase of the cycle, monochrome television will be clearly identified later as properly belonging to the mature phase.

Fortunately, cases of the kind mentioned above appear to be comparatively rare. Products classified as belonging to a particular sector seem to be fairly homogeneous from the point of view of maturity. Difficulties rooted in the fact that the classification system which the Government statistician uses is not perfectly suited to the researcher's needs are bound to arise whenever aggregate data collected for a variety of purposes are used in the analysis of specific problems. The alternative to using such data is to work on more limited statistics collected specifically for a particular purpose. In this case it is felt that meaningful and useful conclusions may be drawn from the aggregate data despite their

---

[1] See page 72 for a brief discussion of the term 'maturity' in the context of this study.

shortcomings. It is deemed preferable, in short, to put up with minor errors arising out of misclassification, the alternative being to base the conclusions on a very limited number of observations.

The above remarks do *not* apply to products belonging to the first phase of the product cycle. Products which have not yet attained widespread distribution are unlikely to figure prominently in the statistical reports of their industry. Information about new products will probably be hidden in the 'other' or 'miscellaneous' groups where the pertinent figures are inseparable from those of numerous unrelated statistics. The Bureau of Census, for example, assigned a special classification to the semiconductor group only in 1963,[1] several years *after* the revolutionary impact of semi-conductors on the electronics industry had become common knowledge.[2] Consequently, one cannot expect to identify a product as belonging to the early phase of the cycle on the basis of sector-wide statistics. The discussion of the characteristics and performance of first-phase industries will therefore be deferred until the next chapter.

The performance of the various sectors of the U.S. electronics industry in the world markets, and their ability to expand sales abroad and to resist the encroachment of foreign supplies on their market share at home, is examined in the following section.

C. THE INTERNATIONAL PERFORMANCE OF THE U.S. ELECTRONICS INDUSTRY

Numerous measures may be used to gauge the international competitive strength of an industry; share of the world markets or a particular segment thereof, share of the domestic market, trends in exports and imports, comparative production costs, all are indicative of the competitive strength possessed by the industry under consideration. For the present purpose, it is proposed to measure the international competitiveness of the U.S. electronics industry by comparing the exports of the industry's various sectors with imports of competing products, and by examining developments in the trade balance of each sector over a period of time.

The trade balance as a measure of competitiveness has of course

[1] *Views*, p. 11.
[2] See for example W. B. Harris, 'The Battle of the Components', *Fortune* (May 1957).

its weaknesses. Imports of a product or groups of products, in the manufacture of which the U.S. has no competitive advantage whatsoever, may well be zero or negligible because of high tariff protection. A rigorous measurement of competitiveness under such conditions would require an item-by-item cost comparison. Strictly speaking, even a comparison of landed costs of imports with the ex-factory price of locally manufactured goods would not yield a satisfactory measure of competitiveness. It was noted in Chapter III that the marketing costs of the exporter may be considerably higher than those incurred by the local manufacturer. Hence only price comparison at the retail level will give a completely satisfactory measure for the purpose at hand. Such comparisons, needless to say, are not readily available, and to the extent that they have been made they cover by necessity only a very small number of items. Some crude cost comparisons between U.S.-made and imported goods will indeed be made in the next chapter. These examples, however, can hardly be regarded as indicative of the broad sector-wide trends which the present section seeks to examine.

It must be realized that aggregate statistics covering many thousands of items are simply not amenable to cost comparisons. Consider, for example, a relatively homogeneous group such as radios. The U.S. Department of Commerce reports the imports of radios, and even breaks them down into transistorized and other types. One could arrive at an average price of imported radios by dividing the number of units into dollar volume. The figures, however, will be quite meaningless unless certain very stringent assumptions about the composition of the imports can be made. It is necessary to assume, for example, that the same ratio of high- and low-priced radios is imported into the country throughout the period under consideration. It must be further assumed that the composition of local production with which imports are compared is similar to that of imports. This assumption is even less warranted than the former, since there is no *a priori* reason to expect that exporters will seek to compete with local firms in the manufacturing of close substitutes. It is more likely, as a matter of fact, that they will try to differentiate their products from those which are manufactured in the importing country. In summary, it is impossible, or at any rate very difficult, to make a meaningful price comparison on the basis of industry-wide trade returns.

Despite its weaknesses an analysis of the dollar volume of exports and imports can be quite useful. In the first place, it is proposed to gauge international competitiveness by analysing trends in trade balances. If trade regulations do not change over the period under consideration, and the trade balance shows a definite pattern, it is possible to make certain deductions about the competitiveness of the industry sector being examined. Improvement in the balance is indicative of a better competitive position and vice versa. In the second place, exports as well as imports have to be considered. It is conceivable that the 'Buy American' Act prevents U.S. firms from buying certain supplies from Japan, even though they would like to do so on the basis of price and quality considerations. The same regulation, however, cannot help the U.S. manufacturers to sell their products abroad. If the U.S. manages to maintain a consistent and significant trade surplus in a given group of products one might justifiably conclude that the country is indeed competitive in their manufacture. If this were not the case, importers would tend to buy their requirements from third countries which are more competitive than the U.S.

Trade figures for five of the six electronics industry sectors, including exports, imports of competing products, and the trade balance, are shown in Table IV(2). Only incomplete data are available for the sixth sector—cathode ray tubes—since imports were not separately reported by the U.S. Department of Commerce prior to October 1963.

Most significant amongst these indicators is the trade balance, which measures the net international position of the sectors being considered and is computed by subtracting imports from exports.

Three of the sectors, Government and industrial products, special-purpose tubes, and components and accessories, had a favourable trade balance throughout the four-year period. Their exports exceeded imports of competitive products by a substantial margin in every one of the years under review. The remaining sectors did significantly worse. The consumer products sector had an unfavourable balance throughout the period. A moderate surplus of the receiving tubes sector in 1960 was turned into a substantial deficit in subsequent years. While the last sector—cathode ray tubes—is known to have had a favourable trade balance during the four-year period, its competitive strength appears to have been seriously eroded, as is evidenced by the drastic change in the

TABLE IV(2)

U.S. Balance of Trade in Selected Electronic Product Groups 1960–3 (*in $ million*)

	Import	Export	Balance	Import	Export	Balance
	Govt'l & Ind'l Products			Consumer Products		
1960	13.2	202.9	189.7	80.0	58.2	(21.8)
1961	17.4	249.9	232.5	98.1	72.0	(26.1)
1962	38.0	336.9	298.9	134.2	74.9	(59.3)
1963	41.4	338.7	297.3	159.4	75.7	(83.7)
% change 1960–3	214	67	57	98	30	(284)
	Special–Purpose Tubes			Receiving Tubes		
1960	2.4	21.6	19.2	10.6	14.4	3.8
1961	3.8	22.0	18.2	13.9	16.4	2.5
1962	3.4	24.1	20.7	22.9	13.8	(9.1)
1963	4.5	25.9	21.4	24.2	12.4	(11.8)
% change 1960–3	88	20	11	128	(14)	—
	Components & Accessories			All Electronic Manufactures		
1960	32.5	89.6	57.2	138.7	408.0	269.3
1961	41.5	113.1	71.6	174.8	494.7	319.9
1962	65.7	137.6	71.9	264.3	603.5	339.2
1963	60.1	161.4	101.3	289.7	624.1	334.4
% change 1960–3	85	80	77	110	53	24

Imports: F.O.B. Origin; Exports: U.S. Value   Negative figures are denoted by brackets.

Export of cathode ray tubes declined from $21.3 million in 1960 to an estimated $10.1 million in 1963. Import figures were not separately recorded prior to October 1963. It appears that the U.S. has an export surplus. 1963 figures were estimated on the basis of trade returns for the first eleven months of the year.

Source: *Views*, Appendix, Table XVIII.

sector's exports, which declined by over 50 per cent between 1960 and 1963.

The comparative performance of the individual sectors might be best gauged by the *trends* exhibited by their exports, imports, and trade balances over a period of time. Percentage changes in the level of these indicators, which were computed for the 1960–3 period, are given in the table.[1]

Two sectors, Government and industrial products and components and accessories, improved their trade surplus substantially between 1960 and 1963. Special-purpose tubes, the third sector with a large favourable balance, managed to hold its own, but did not improve its position appreciably. The trade balance of the remaining sectors deteriorated over the period, and the deterioration appears to have gathered momentum during the last two years. The deficit of the consumer products sector quadrupled between 1960 and 1963, and the surplus which receiving tubes enjoyed as late as 1961 turned into a substantial deficit in the following year. By 1963, imports of the sector were twice as high as its exports.

Judging by their international performance, the six sectors may in summary be divided into two distinct groups. Decisive competitive strength was exhibited by the first group, which includes Government and industrial products, components and accessories, and, to a lesser degree, special-purpose tubes. The trade balance of these sectors improved appreciably between 1960 and 1963. Unmistakable deterioration in the trade balance characterized the performance of the second group, which includes the consumer products, receiving tubes, and cathode ray tube sectors.

Having identified the sectors of the industry by their international performance it is next necessary to classify them on the basis of their relative maturity in order to test the proposition that the two factors are correlated.

D. MATURITY

The discussion in the previous section showed that three sectors out of the six into which the U.S. electronics industry is commonly

---

[1] Choice of a base period for the purpose of establishing the existence of trends is of course arbitrary to some extent, and may at times give rise to distortions. The trends which are indicated by the figures shown in the table appear nevertheless to be quite firm, and no change in the computation method could alter their direction.

divided exhibited considerable competitive strength internationally, whereas the other three appeared to lose ground to their foreign competitors. The components and accessories, Government and industrial products, and special-purpose tubes sectors improved their positive trade balance between 1960 and 1963. On the other hand, the trade balance of goods manufactured by the consumer products, receiving tubes, and cathode ray tubes sectors deteriorated considerably during the same period. In order to accept the proposition that the U.S. possesses a competitive advantage in new products, while having a disadvantage in mature ones, it is necessary to show that the first three sectors listed above are less mature than the remaining sectors.

The product-cycle model suggests that the maturity of different industries is manifested by the trend of their output. Significant increases in output characterize growth industries, whereas mature industries may be identified by sluggish growth or declining output.[1] Maturity, however, is necessarily a relative concept whose applicability to different industries may vary from one instant to another. For the purpose at hand, it is proposed to gauge the

TABLE IV(3)

Value Added, Principal Electronics Industry Groups,
Selected Years 1947–62 ($ millions)

Industry Year	All Electronics	Gov't and Indust'l	Spec. Purpose Tubes	Compon'ts and Accessories	Consumer Products	Rec'g & Cathode Ray Tubes
1947	794	137	18	198	365	76
1954	2,624	734	106	701	712	322
1958	3,325	1,298	166	915	594	353
1959	4,247	1,523	201	1,383	727	406
1960	4,776	1,968	203	1,533	694	377
1961	5,289	2,400	225	1,619	729	315
1962	6,435	3,013	273	1,977	869	302
Annual per cent changes (compound)						
1947–62	15.0	22.9	19.9	16.6	6.0	9.6
1947–54	18.6	27.8	28.8	20.3	10.0	22.9
1954–58	6.1	14.2	11.9	6.1	(4.4)	2.3
1958–62	17.9	23.4	13.2	21.2	10.0	(3.7)

Source: *Views*, pp. 15, 45.

[1] See Chapter II.

maturity of the different sectors of the U.S. electronics industry by comparing the rates at which their respective value added changed over the fifteen-year period 1947–62.[1] Table IV(3) shows the growth rates exhibited by the industry's principal sectors. Annual average rates for selective periods are calculated in the lower part of the table.[2]

TABLE IV(4)

Growth Rate, Principal Electronics Industry Groups:
Ratio Analysis of Indices 1947 = 100

Year	Total Industry Index	Government and Industrial Products Index	Index Ratio (a)	Special–Purpose Tubes Index	Index Ratio (a)
1947	100	100	100	100	100
1954	331	558	160	588	178
1958	418	947	226	922	220
1959	535	1112	208	1116	208
1960	602	1436	238	1127	187
1961	666	1752	263	1250	188
1962	810	2198	271	1517	187

Year	Components and Accessories Index	Index Ratio (a)	Consumer Products Index	Index Ratio (a)	Receiving and Cathode Ray Tubes Index	Index Ratio (a)
1947	100	100	100	100	100	100
1954	365	110	196	59	424	128
1958	463	111	163	39	464	111
1959	701	132	200	37	534	100
1960	774	129	191	32	496	82
1961	817	123	200	32	414	62
1962	998	123	238	29	397	49

(a) Index of the particular industry divided by the index of all electronics industries.

Source: Table V (3).

[1] A 10 per cent annual growth rate may be considered high in one industry and moderate in another. The analysis, however, does not seek to measure the performance of the electronics industry against that of the whole economy. By comparing the growth of the sectors to each other it is possible to establish an industry-wide yardstick by which growth sectors can be distinguished from mature ones.

[2] The data on the receiving tube and cathode ray tube sectors were reported together in *Views*. Having failed to obtain separate data reported on a consistent basis from other sources, the writer decided to present the available data in its present form.

Value added of three sectors, Government and industrial products, special-purpose tubes, and components and accessories, increased faster than industry as a whole. Of these sectors, Government and industrial products increased at the highest rate throughout the period. The consumer products sector, which was the largest in 1947, was overtaken by Government and industrial products as well as by components and accessories in the early fifties. The growth rate of the sector was negative during the 1954–61 period. The receiving and cathode ray tubes sector, which is the principal supplier of the consumer products sector, was by far the weakest. Value added amounted to over $400 million in 1959. It actually declined steadily in subsequent years, despite the upswing which the rest of the industry experienced.

A more detailed analysis of comparative growth rates is presented in Table IV(4). A value added index using 1947 as a base year is compiled for the whole industry and for each sector. Next, the index of the whole industry is divided into that of each sector. The resulting *index ratio* enables the reader to judge the extent to which a sector is running ahead of the industry as a whole or, conversely, the extent to which it is trailing behind.[1]

Judged by the rate of their expansion, and by their comparative

---

[1] These indices of the rise in value do not allow for price changes. However, the difference in growth rates between the three rapidly growing sectors and the rest is so marked, over the whole period 1947-62, that it would almost certainly show up in volume indices as well, if these were available. Corrections for price changes can be made to four of the sectors for the period 1957-9 to 62; the consequential changes in growth rates are not substantial. The main difference is that the output of special-purpose tubes, which during this period rose a little faster than the output of consumer products when measured in value terms, rose a little more slowly when measured in volume terms:-

	Price index 1962	Annual per cent change (compounds) in value added in	
	1957-9 = 100	Value terms	Volume terms
Special-purpose tubes	103	+13.2	+12.5
Consumer products	88	+10.0	+13.5
Cathode ray tubes	102	− 1.5	− 1.0
Radio and receiving tubes	99	− 4.3	− 4.1

Source: *Views*, Tables III, V, VI, VII.

position relative to the whole industry, Government and industrial products, components and accessories, and special-purpose tubes should be classified as growth sectors. These sectors increased their value added tenfold or more during the 1947–62 period. More significantly, their high growth rate was not restricted to the early part of the period. After 1954 all three sectors more than doubled their value added, which rose in every year listed in the table above the level of the preceding one. When measured in relation to the performance of the whole industry, the value added of the three sectors increased at a faster rate than the average. The consumer products and receiving and cathode ray tubes sectors exhibited, by contrast, the characteristics of mature industries. While the value added of these sectors increased between 1947 and 1962, the bulk of their growth was restricted to the early part of the period. Value added of the consumer products increased little after 1954, and that of receiving and cathode ray tubes actually declined. Moreover, the deterioration in their relative position has been steady and consistent in the second half of the period and shows no sign of coming to a halt.

The above figures suggest that a negative correlation appears to exist between the maturity of the various sectors of the U.S. electronics industry and their international performance. Those sectors which had a high growth rate improved their trade balance, whereas the slow-growing or declining sectors have been losing ground to foreign competition. These findings are consistent with the predictions of the product-cycle model.

It may be argued at this point that correlation between the maturity of the U.S. electronics industry and its international performance could conceivably be attributed to the impact of imports on the output of the domestic industry. Other things being equal, the domestic production of an industry will be sluggish if imports displace local production. The cause and effect relationship claimed by the model for maturity and international competitiveness may then be reversed; international competitiveness being the cause, and maturity the effect.

Changes in the output rate of an industry may be attributed to foreign competition under one of the following conditions:

(1) when imports displace local manufactures in the domestic market;

(2) when foreign manufactures displace exports.

In either case, the volume of foreign trade must be significant in order to affect the output rate of the industry in question. If imports are small in comparison with domestic consumption, even a considerable increase in imports will have little effect on the output rate of the domestic industry. Similarly, if exports account for only a small proportion of the industry's output, wide changes in the volume of exports will have only a marginal effect on the industry output rate. This indeed appears to have been the case of the U.S. electronics industry.

The consumer products and receiving tubes sectors were identified above as mature sectors because of the low or negative rate at which their output was changing. Table IV(5) below indicates

TABLE IV(5)

U.S. Output and Imports of Electronic Consumer Products and Receiving Tubes ($ million)

	1958	1960	1962	Annual per cent changes (compound) 1958–62
Consumer products				
Output	1,516	1,737	1,906	+5.9
Imports	17	80	134	
Output plus imports	1,533	1,817	2,040	+7.4
Receiving tubes				
Output	383	397	310	−5.2
Imports	5	11	23	
Output plus imports	388	408	333	−3.7

Source: *Views*, Statistical Appendix, Tables V, VI, and XVI.

the extent to which imports might have retarded the output of these sectors.[1] The table, which shows imports side by side with domestic output, suggests what the output of the two sectors might have been had imports been displaced by local production.[2]

The figures suggest that if imports of consumer products were

[1] Import figures for the third mature sector—cathode ray tubes—are unavailable.
[2] The table is constructed on the assumption that the elasticity of demand for import products or their domestic substitutes is unity. If price of these products goes up by 1 per cent, quantity demanded falls by 1 per cent. Total sales volume thus remains unchanged.

replaced by added domestic output, average annual change in output would have risen from 5.9 per cent to 7.4 per cent. The additional output would not have sufficed to change the position of the sector in comparison with that of the growth sectors, whose output rose at a considerably higher rate during the same period, as Tables IV(3) and IV(4) show. The table also shows that the decline in the output of the receiving tubes sector could not possibly be attributed to foreign competition. If the domestic industry had supplied 100 per cent of the domestic market, output would have still declined from $388 million to $333 million.[1]

There remains the possibility that the growth rate of the two sectors was retarded by foreign competition in the export markets. If this were to be the case, failure of the U.S. industry to be competitive in the world markets could be said to be responsible for the decline of the growth rate of the sectors' output. This possibility, however, is quite remote considering the marginal importance of exports to the U.S. electronics industry. In 1960, for example, exports of receiving tubes and consumer products accounted for 3 per cent of total output. Even if exports had been 50 per cent or 100 per cent higher, they would have failed to change the trend in the output rate of the two sectors.

Finally, it is necessary to consider the absolute size of the U.S. market, which, as recently as 1963, accounted for nearly 60 per cent of the free world's output of electronic products.[2] While *foreign* demand may be growing at a high rate, *total* demand as viewed by the U.S. industry is, of course, highly influenced by trends in the domestic market. Consequently, even if U.S. exporters manage to maintain their market share abroad, total output of the industry will be only marginally affected.

In summary, it is unlikely that foreign competition did significantly affect the output rate of the consumer products and the receiving tubes sectors. The previous growth in the output of the two sectors could not have been maintained, even if foreign competition were less formidable. It must be concluded, therefore, that foreign competition cannot be said to be the cause of the correlation found between the international performance of the consumer goods and receiving tubes sectors and their maturity.

[1] Competition from semiconductors and saturation of the market appear to have been responsible for the change in the growth rate of the two sectors.
[2] Electronic Industries Association, *Electronic Industries Yearbook 1964* (Washington, 1964), p. 59.

E. THE MANUFACTURING PROCESS

It is of some interest to see whether the two groups of electronic products—those in the growth phase and those in the mature phase—show the expected product-cycle characteristics in other ways, as well as in international trade. One would expect the growth sectors to employ more skill-intensive methods and the mature sectors to be more capital-intensive now than they were when in the growth phase.

One would not expect to find that every product in the mature phase was produced in a more capital-intensive way than any product in the growth phase. The steel industry, for example, was probably more capital-intensive than the textile industry in all the phases through which both industries passed. What the product-cycle view suggests is that for any particular product the ratio of the capital stock to value added will be higher in the mature than in the growth phase. To demonstrate this, figures are needed of the capital employed throughout the life-cycle of the same product. Figures of this kind are not normally available, because it is often only at a fairly late stage in the growth phase that the product becomes sufficiently important to be separately distinguished in the statistics.

However, within the electronics industry there are basic similarities in the technology of the various industry groups; radar equipment, radio and television sets, and computers are all assembled from a comparatively limited range of component families which have many common characteristics. It is therefore probably reasonable to attribute significant variations in the manufacturing processes of the various electronic product groups to different phases of maturity. In other words, it is suggested here that if the production processes of the fast-growing sectors of the U.S. electronics industry are found to be more labour and skill-intensive and less capital-intensive than the processes used by the slow-growing sectors, this finding should be regarded as being in accordance with expectations derived from the product-cycle model. This does in fact appear to be the case. The receiving tubes sector has been described in a recent survey as manufacturing 'standardized size and types of tubes at competitive prices requiring large capital investment in plant and equipment'.[1] The consumer

---

[1] *Views*, p. 135.

products sector has been similarly described as manufacturing items which are 'generally mass-produced, using automatic mechanized processes'.[1] The processes commonly used in military and industrial equipment manufacturing are described by contrast as 'not as highly mechanized as electronic components and consumer product plants ... fabrication and assembly operations are difficult to mechanize because of the relatively short production runs and frequent design changes'.[2]

The expectations derived from the product-cycle model are also borne out in comparisons of the skill intensity of the methods of production. One would expect the growth sectors to employ a higher proportion of skilled people than the mature sectors. This is what the employment situation in the industry shows. In all three growth sectors there is a much higher proportion of non-production workers than in any of the mature sectors (Table IV(6)). Indeed, in the Government and industrial sector nearly half the employees are non-production workers, as against only one-fifth in the consumer products and other mature sectors. Where this proportion is high, the input of scientific and engineering skill is high as well.[3]

The present section on the manufacturing process can be best summarized by the following quotation:

> The manufacture of military and space products, and to a lesser extent of industrial and commercial products, involves a great deal of research and development work and low volume production of custom-made end products, and requires relatively large proportions of professional and other highly trained workers. In comparison, the manufacture of consumer products and components tends to be an assembly line-mass production operation involving relatively large proportions of semi skilled and manufacturing workers.[4]

F. SUMMARY

The statistics and analysis of the preceding sections present a consistent pattern of the international competitiveness of the U.S.

---

[1] U.S. Bureau of Labor Statistics, *Employment Outlook and Changing Occupational Structure in Electronic Manufacturing* (Washington, Government Printing Office, 1963), p. 5.

[2] U.S. Business and Defence Services Administration, *The United States Industrial Outlook for 1963*, E.R.-63 (Washington, Government Printing Office, 1963).

[3] *Views*, page 12: 'A high proportion of non-production workers is engaged in research and development.'

[4] Bureau of Labor Statistics, op. cit., p. 2.

TABLE IV(6)

*U.S. Electronics Industry: Proportions of Production and
Non-Production Workers, 1958–62*

Thousands

	1958	1962	Annual per cent change (compound)
GROWTH PRODUCTS			
GOVERNMENT AND INDUSTRIAL			
Total employment, of which	129.5	282.6	21.5
Production workers	78.1	147.9	17.3
Non-production workers	51.4	134.7	27.2
Per cent of non-production workers	**39.7**	**47.7**	
SPECIAL-PURPOSE TUBES			
Total employment, of which	20.4	24.8	5.0
Production workers	14.5	15.2	1.2
Non-production workers	5.7	9.6	13.9
Per cent of non-production workers	**27.9**	**38.7**	
COMPONENTS AND ACCESSORIES			
Total employment, of which	132.2	237.9	15.8
Production workers	102.9	169.7	13.3
Non-production workers	29.4	68.2	23.4
Per cent of non-production workers	**22.2**	**28.7**	
MATURE PRODUCTS			
CONSUMER PRODUCTS			
Total employment, of which	66.5	82.9	5.7
Production workers	52.0	66.0	6.1
Non-production workers	14.5	16.9	3.9
Per cent of non-production workers	**21.8**	**20.4**	
RECEIVING TUBES			
Total employment, of which	36.9	26.6	−7.9
Production workers	30.9	21.4	−8.8
Non-production workers	6.0	5.2	−3.5
Per cent of non-production workers	**16.3**	**19.5**	
CATHODE RAY TUBES			
Total employment, of which	8.6	6.8	−5.7
Production workers	7.0	5.4	−6.3
Non-production workers	1.6	1.4	−3.3
Per cent of non-production workers	**18.6**	**20.6**	

Source: *Views*, Statistical Appendix, Tables I–VII, Census Data.

electronics industry. Those sectors which have experienced a high growth rate in recent years have exhibited considerable strength internationally. The international performance of the slow-growing and sluggish sectors has been weak by contrast. Table IV(7) shows in summary form how the international performance of the different sectors is related to their growth rate and to the major characteristics of the production process which they have adopted.

TABLE IV(7)

Summary of Changes in the Growth Rate, Manufacturing Characteristics, and Trade Balance of the Principal Sectors of the U.S. Electronics Industry

% changes in: *	% change	rank	% change	rank	% change	rank
Sector	Gov't & Industrial		Components & Accessories		Special-Purpose Tubes	
Value added	131	1	116	2	64	3
No. production workers	89	1	65	2	5	3
No. non-production workers	162	1	132	2	68	3
1963 index of trade balance 1960=100	157	2	177	1	111	3
	Consumer Products		Cathode Ray Tubes		Receiving Tubes	
Value added	46	4	(6)	5	(16)	6
No. production workers	27	4	(12)	5	(31)	6
No. non-production workers	17	4	(12)	5	(13)	6
1963 index of trade balance 1960=100	(384)	4	(a)	–	n.a.	–

* All changes are for the 1958-62 period, unless specifically stated otherwise
(a) Balance turned from positive to negative
Source: Tables IV (2), IV (3), and IV (6); *Views*, Appendix, Tables VI and VII.

The table lists the changes in growth rate, expenditures, employment of production and non-production workers, and international competitiveness which the various sectors of the industry have experienced during the 1958–62 or 1960–3 period. These changes are first expressed in percentage points and are then translated into ranks, with the highest percentage change getting rank 1, the second highest rank 2, &c. The sectors were listed in the order of their ranking in value added. The Government and industrial electronics sector was listed first, the components and accessories sector second, the special-purpose tubes sector third, &c.

The table points clearly and unambiguously to the existence of a high degree of correlation between the measures which were used to indicate growth, labour and skill intensity, and international competitiveness.

Government and industrial products, components and accessories, and special-purpose tubes, which were identified as growth sectors, have been given low ranks in all four categories. The ranking of the consumer products, cathode ray tubes, and receiving tubes sectors has been similarly consistent. These mature sectors are given high ranks in all categories. This remarkable degree of correlation is consistent with the hypothesis that competitive strength in the U.S. industry is associated with high growth rate, and that both are found in industries which are labour and skill-intensive. A weakening competitive position, on the other hand, is associated with a capital-intensive production process and comparatively little use of scientific and engineering labour inputs.

The findings suggest that the competitive advantage which the U.S. has in electronic products is dynamic in nature. As specific product groups assume more mature characteristics, as the production process becomes more stable, as the specifications become more standardized, and the importance of the skill content declines, foreign manufacturers are likely to import the production technology, adapt it to their environment, and, in time, provide stiff competition to U.S. manufacturers in their own market.

V

THE INTERNATIONAL COMPETITIVENESS OF FIRST-PHASE PRODUCTS: AN EMPIRICAL ANALYSIS

A. INTRODUCTION

THE findings of the previous chapter were consistent with the proposition that the U.S. has a comparative advantage in the manufacture of new products. No distinction was made, however, between products belonging to what have been termed in the study the first and second phases of the product cycle. All comparatively new products were lumped together under the heading of growth products, and their competitiveness was compared to that of mature ones.

The purpose of the present chapter is to examine in detail empirical evidence concerning the factors which specifically affect the international competitiveness of products belonging to the early phase of the product cycle. The manufacturing process and marketing function of first-phase products were shown in Chapters II and III to be unique in several respects. The essential points made in these chapters are briefly restated here.

A high degree of labour-intensity characterizes the manufacturing process. The small size of the market, its volatility, and the necessity to change frequently the specifications and methods of production preclude the adoption of more capital-intensive methods suitable for longer runs and more uniform outputs. The composition of the labour force is especially significant. Scientists, engineers, and skilled labourers assume a role of crucial importance, since their professional skills are required to cope with the many problems of design and engineering which inevitably accompany the introduction of new products.

The manufacturer often depends heavily on supplies, services, and specialized skills obtained from other firms. The importance of these external economies was clearly demonstrated in the New York regional study cited in Chapter III.[1] That study showed how numerous manufacturers of new products are attracted to the New York metropolitan region, despite its high labour costs, exorbitant rents, and congested traffic conditions, because of the generous external economies which the region offers. The study also demonstrated that the importance of external economies decreases directly (though at different rates which vary from product to product) with the maturity of the industries utilizing them. As products become more mature, and as the scale of manufacture assumes larger proportions, it becomes more economical for the manufacturer to provide a growing range of services internally, rather than to rely on outsiders to supply them.

Finally, it is necessary to consider the marketing function. It was argued in Chapter III that the foreign manufacturer will always have a certain disadvantage as far as marketing costs are concerned. It was stated further that the degree of his disadvantage is a function of the maturity of the products he handles. The less mature the product, the more pronounced his handicap. Examples of the special hurdles which the exporter has to overcome in order to compete effectively with the local manufacturer include the necessity of providing the buyers with complex services and of maintaining extensive communications with them. The complexity and costs involved in fulfilling these functions increase substantially with distance, as will be shown later.

Some of the factors discussed above strengthen the competitive position of U.S.-based manufacturers, whereas others tend to weaken it. Protected by distance, Government regulations, and tariffs, the U.S.-based local manufacturer has access on preferential terms to a large home market. Internal demand for new first-phase products is sustained by the size and affluence of the country in general, and by its huge defence and space programmes in particular. As far as supply of production factors is concerned, the U.S. manufacturer has access to a large reservoir of scientific and engineering talents. Moreover, he is better placed than his foreign competitors to benefit from external economies, since the array of supplies and technical, scientific, and financial services available in the U.S. is undoubtedly unmatched elsewhere.

High employment costs, on the other hand, affect the competitive

[1] Hall (ed.), *Made in New York.*

position of the U.S. adversely. Certain countries such as Britain, Switzerland, and Israel are, like the U.S., relatively well endowed with engineers and scientists. Employment costs in these countries are, however, well below the U.S. level. Consequently, they may have a competitive edge in certain first-phase products which are characterized by a high proportion of scientific and human inputs on the one hand, and by little dependence on external economies on the other.

The considerations mentioned above led to the formulation of the following hypotheses regarding the international competitiveness of first-phase products:

(1) The competitive advantage enjoyed by the U.S. in the manufacture of new products in general does not necessarily extend to all first-phase products. Certain product groups may be manufactured at less cost in other countries.

(2) The adverse effect of proposition (1) on the competitive position of U.S. manufacturers in their home market is minimized owing to the difficulties involved in the marketing of first-phase products across national borders.

The methods used to test the validity of these propositions are determined by the nature of the products and the available information. Published industry-wide statistical data are useless for the purpose at hand. Statistics on first-phase products which have, by definition, a small market are not publicly available in sufficiently detailed form. Consequently it is necessary to rely on information obtained in individual case studies. The usefulness of the latter method is further enhanced by the detailed information about the production process and marketing methods which a case study can generate. Without such information it is difficult to identify and analyse in a meaningful way the factors which determine the international competitiveness of first-phase products.

The hypotheses advanced above are tested on data pertaining to synthetic crystals, a group of products with widespread applications in the electronics industry, and whose manufacture requires a high degree of scientific skill. Production and marketing costs and operating problems of a hypothetical U.S. crystals producer and a foreign-based competitor are compared in the following sections. The foreign manufacturer is assumed to be located in Israel, which was identified above as a country comparatively well endowed with scientific and engineering skills.

B. SYNTHETIC CRYSTALS—THEIR USES, DEVELOPMENT, AND ECONOMIC CHARACTERISTICS[1]

Synthetic crystals are chemical compounds most commonly 'grown' from a melt under carefully controlled conditions designed to ensure that the product will have the desired chemical composition, molecular structure, and optical characteristics. Crystals are used to control the flow of electro-magnetic waves of different characteristics. They are utilized in a great variety of applications ranging from transistors through optics to lasers. The best-known commercial crystals are semiconductors such as germanium and silicon. They form the core of transistors, diodes, and other electronic components that have facilitated several revolutionary developments in the electronics industry during the last fifteen years. Numerous crystals are used in scintillation (detection and measurement of radiation), X-ray, infra-red and ultra-violet equipment. Several models of lasers also utilize a variety of crystals.

A good deal of the basic research and development work on new crystals is done in academic institutions. The Massachusetts Institute of Technology, for example, which maintains two large and well staffed crystal-growing laboratories, is a leader in crystals development. Other laboratories are maintained by the armed forces and several large companies such as American Telephone and Telegraph, General Electric, and Radio Corporation of America.

The bulk of development financing comes from Government agencies, which place development contracts with the various laboratories. The results of the work performed with Government financing are, as a rule, made public property, and commercial crystal growers may use the information made available in this fashion.

Some development work is performed by commercial growers for their customers. The sales brochure of one crystal grower— Semi Elements—claims that 'Our insight into the secrets of nature has become so acute that Semi-Elements will accept orders on a firm basis and with confidence, for crystals never before grown'. Such work is possible because the equipment used for development work is essentially the same as that required for commercial

[1] See appendix at the end of the chapter for sources of data and methodology.

production. Moreover, since many crystals are grown to strict specifications and sold in small quantities, it is often difficult to distinguish between development work and full scale production.

Impetus for new developments often comes from the universities. Several of the newer, more exotic crystals were developed in response to research needs in microwave physics, nuclear physics, and other branches of the sciences. They are used as windows, lenses, prisms, and other components in specialized equipment or measurement devices. The bulk of this type of equipment has defence and space applications and is used to satisfy needs for sophisticated measuring, tracking, and tracing devices.

Certain crystals gain access to wider commercial markets when they get incorporated in industrial control, radiation detection, or medical equipment. Most crystals never reach this status, since the demand for the equipment of which they form a part is small. Others enjoy a brief spell of 'popularity', and then disappear as better substitutes are developed.

The market for standard crystals such as silicon and germanium is both large and relatively stable, in comparison with the laser, scintillation, IR (infra-red), and UV (ultra-violet) crystals market, which is small and extremely volatile. The composition and size of the newer crystals market are constantly shifting owing to technological innovations, which make certain crystals redundant while creating new demand for others. While it is, of course, difficult to generalize about a field which contains so many sub-groups, there is little doubt that the life-cycle of most crystals is relatively short. This is particularly true of crystals which are used in new applications such as lasers.

Obsolescence may occasionally cast its shadow in the form of entirely new materials. A case in point is the appearance of Irtran, a material having infra-red applications developed by Kodak a few years ago. Irtran differs from single crystals in that it is made of polycrystalline materials and is pressed rather than individually grown. It lends itself readily to cutting and polishing and is therefore preferable to certain crystals which are very difficult to fabricate. While Irtran has gained market acceptance, it has not, by any means, revolutionized or pre-empted the field. The company prints a pertinent remark on its loose-leaf file type of catalogue: 'Infra-red developments move too fast for a bound catalog. Kodak will supply new sheets as new data and new products come along.'

Economic rather than technical constraints appear to be responsible for the choice of crystal-growing technology. Specifications for silicon crystals, for example, have become sufficiently standardized, and the size of the market has expanded enough in recent years, to justify the introduction of continuous-process production methods. The bulk of the remaining crystals are manufactured by a process which is more reminiscent of home cooking than of industrial production.

Crystals are commonly grown by methods known as the Stockbarger or Bridgeman methods. A machined graphite crucible containing carefully mixed chemicals is placed in an electrical furnace, which is hermetically sealed and then pumped down to create a vacuum. The vacuum is necessary to prevent undesirable chemical reaction from occurring. It ensures maximum purity, which is crucial for the quality of the crystal. Electricity is next turned on, and the material is melted slowly. After melting has been achieved, at temperatures ranging from 400° to 1,500° Centigrade, depending on the chemical compounds used, the growing process begins. The crucible is lowered very slowly below the area of maximum heat, and crystal formation begins to take place in the cooler parts of the crucible. During the cooling phases, stresses in the structure may occur; and if the temperature is not properly controlled the crystals may be useless for practical applications.

The growth cycle varies in length from a few hours to several weeks, depending on the volume. Crystals having a diameter of one inch can be grown at the rate of approximately four millimetres per hour. Fifteen-inch-long crystals with a diameter of ten inches take from three to four weeks to grow. The furnaces used for growing large crystals are considerably larger in size than those required for the smaller ones.

The qualifications of the labour force determine more than any other single factor the quality and value of the crystals which a manufacturer is capable of producing. Chemists are required to evaluate, purify, mix, and test the ingredients which constitute the raw materials. Successful crystal growing is dependent on the proper preparation of these ingredients, which cannot be obtained, as a rule, in sufficiently pure form from commercial sources. Most defects found in crystals are attributable in the last resort to faulty raw material preparation. The experience, training, and skill of the chemists are consequently the major factors which determine both quality and productivity.

Other skilled persons needed are machinists, who turn the fragile graphite crucibles containing the raw materials, and technicians, who supervise and maintain the furnaces and the vacuum systems. Unskilled labourers, sorters, and helpers make up the remainder of the production personnel. The total size of the latter depends on the scale of the operation and the kind of crystals grown. As the scale increases the proportion of the professional employees tends to fall, since each professional can direct the work of several less skilled or unskilled people. A crystals grower specializing in standard crystals will similarly require a lower proportion of skilled people than a grower of special crystals.

Manufacturing equipment consists mainly, as was noted above, of electrical furnaces equipped with vacuum systems. Annealing furnaces are also required for the purpose of relieving the structural stresses of the crystals. Ancillary equipment consists of chemical testing and measuring equipment, a mechanical lathe for turning the crucibles, and other miscellaneous pieces of equipment for maintenance and routine repairs. Ready access to a chemical laboratory and to a machine shop may obviate the need for most of the ancillary equipment.

Several preliminary conclusions regarding the competitive potential of an Israel-based crystal grower wishing to penetrate the U.S. market are suggested by the above discussion. Leaving aside for the time being marketing problems, it appears that the U.S. manufacturer's biggest advantage lies in the area of development. In order to stay in business, a crystal manufacturer must possess the capability of producing new crystals from time to time. The learning process, which may be long and expensive, can be shortened somewhat by sharing the information and experience accumulated by other growers. Since many of the latter are located in universities and Government-financed institutions, they do as a rule co-operate liberally with commercial firms. The latter, moreover, occasionally benefit from Government-financed development contracts, which help them defray development costs and provide valuable experience for their personnel.[1]

---

[1] Commercial growers whose development work is financed by Government contracts are obliged to make their findings available to the public. These firms tend, however, to publish only the minimum amount of information which their agreements oblige them to divulge.

Lacking a home market, the Israeli manufacturer is denied many of these benefits. The U.S. Government is unlikely to award defence-related development contracts to a foreign firm, and the Israeli Government has practically no need for crystals needed in sophisticated equipment used in connexion with the U.S. space program. While he may have access to information publicly available in the U.S., the cost of obtaining such information will be high for several reasons. In order to familiarize themselves with the latest developments, scientists from Israel will have to make extensive trips to the U.S. Information gathered on occasional visits, moreover, is unlikely to be as useful as the routine contacts which U.S. scientists working for local firms can develop owing to their proximity to the market and to the institutions where important developments occur.

The competitive disadvantages suffered by the Israeli manufacturer in the area of new product development in this field are mitigated by the fact that local academic institutions are actively engaged in crystallography work, and operate crystal-growing laboratories. The Israeli manufacturer may benefit from the experience of these researchers in solving tricky development problems. Testing facilities and important data may be put at his disposal. Above all, the scientists of the universities are likely to keep up with new developments abroad and to stay in close contact with their professional colleagues overseas. The information gathered by them can be shared as a matter of course with commercial crystals facilities.

Manufacturing in Israel solely for the export market would probably be unthinkable in the absence of university-based crystals laboratories. The existence of such facilities can provide an Israeli manufacturer with at least some of the external economies available to his foreign competitors. Since the services of Israeli scientists can be obtained at a fraction of their U.S. employment costs, total manufacturing expenses in Israel are likely to be relatively low. The cost margin could, under certain circumstances, be large enough to compensate the exporter for the extra outlays connected with the marketing of his products. Estimated costs of operating identical crystal-growing companies in the U.S. and in Israel are presented in the next section.

C. COMPARATIVE MANUFACTURING COSTS IN THE U.S. AND IN ISRAEL[1]

Before proceeding with the comparison between the estimated manufacturing costs in Israel and in the U.S. it may be advisable to state the assumptions upon which the comparison is based. These assumptions concern the product mix and the size of the respective facilities. Many possible combinations of size and product mix are technically and economically feasible. It is up to management to decide which types of crystals should be manufactured, and what share of the market the firm should try to control.

For the present purpose only crystals belonging to the halides group will be considered. Halides are chemical compounds based on fluoride, chloride, bromide, or iodide. Crystals belonging to this group are used in three separate though related markets: infra-red and ultra-violet optical instruments, scintillation equipment, and to a small extent laser apparatus. While similar processes are used in the manufacture of both halides and several other crystal families, the marketing problems of the former are sufficiently unique to justify their separate consideration. Finally, certain halide crystals have been grown by Hebrew University scientists for several years, and some of the present cost estimates are based on their experience.

The size of the U.S. market is presently estimated at about $5.5 million. The lion's share is held by Harshaw Chemicals, a diversified chemical company which is believed to control about 80 per cent of the market. Five small companies, whose crystals sales average about $200,000 apiece, share the remaining 20 per cent between them. It is assumed that the annual sales volume of the hypothetical Israeli Company will be equal to the average volume of the smaller U.S. plants. The market is growing at a fast enough rate to absorb an extra $200,000 without causing disruptions in the existing sales volume and price structure. Higher sales by a foreign supplier are likely to be resisted by the local manufacturers, who may clamour for Government protection. A

---

[1] U.S. labour cost estimates are based on the actual experience of several U.S. firms. The outlays of a hypothetical Israeli plant were projected on the basis of the experience of the Hebrew University crystals laboratory and U.S. operating data. The latter were adjusted to take into account relevant industry wage levels prevailing in Israel and other cost factors. For details see Appendix.

smaller sales volume on the other hand is unlikely to be economical in view of the fact that a considerable proportion of the sales revenue must be spent in the U.S. on marketing expenses.

A manufacturing facility capable of producing $200,000 worth of halide crystals per annum requires six to seven furnaces.[1] It is assumed here to employ a direct labour force consisting of two chemists, two technicians, and one helper, all of whom operate under the direction of a general manager. Estimated employment costs in two identical plants located in the U.S. and in Israel are given in table V(1) below.

TABLE V(1)

Manpower Requirements and Comparative Employment Costs in the U.S. and Israeli Plants[2]

Production employees	No.	Employment costs in U.S.	Israel
Manager[3]	½	$ 9,000	$ 3,000
Chemists	2	24,000	8,000
Technicians	2	12,000	5,000
Helpers	1	4,500	1,800
	5½	$49,500	$17,800
Fringe benefits		(20%) 9,900	(30%) 5,400
Total production employment costs		$59,400	$23,200

The pay differential between the two countries is worthy of note. The wages and salaries of the U.S. employees exceed those of their Israeli counterparts by a considerable margin. The margin, however, is by no means uniform. It is largest at the level of the general manager and the chemists and declines gradually with the lower-skilled personnel. This state of affairs can be attributed, in part at least, to the egalitarian tradition of Israel, which regards with disfavour large gaps between the wage levels of different skill groups.

[1] The methodology used to calculate furnace requirements is described in the appendix.
[2] See Appendix for sources of data and for derivation of figures.
[3] The manager is assumed to devote half his time to the supervision of the manufacturing operations, and the remainder to other management functions.

Fringe benefits such as sick pay, annual leave, and social security contributions are reported to account for a higher percentage of wages in Israel than in the U.S. The difference in total employment costs between the two countries is consequently smaller than the gap between the nominal wage rates, as the table shows.

Table V(1) was constructed on the assumption that both firms are going to be equally efficient in the technical sense, i.e. a given combination of inputs is assumed to be capable of producing the same physical quantity of comparable outputs in both plants. Since identical equipment is assumed to be used in the two countries, and since the qualifications of the labour force are strictly specified, there is no reason to expect one operation to be more efficient than the other. The U.S. operation will nevertheless be more efficient than the Israeli one in several important respects. The plant manager in the U.S. will be able to spend a good part of his time on marketing problems. Being physically remote from the market, his Israeli counterpart will be prevented from using his time so effectively. In addition, U.S.-made crystals are going to be cut in the plant, whereas Israeli crystals will be shipped abroad in ingot form to minimize customs duties.[1] The significance of these 'geography determined' efficiency factors will be discussed in more detail in the next section.

Estimates of other manufacturing cost including items such as raw materials and supplies, rent and building maintenance, are shown in Table V(2).

TABLE V(2)

Summary of Material and Manufacturing Overhead Costs[2]

	U.S.	Israel
Raw material	$ 2,600	$ 2,700
Electricity	2,300	1,800
Rent and maintenance	12,000	5,000
Parts and supplies	8,000	10,000
Depreciation	15,000	15,000
	$39,900	$34,500

[1] U.S. customs duties in 1964 amounted to $10\frac{1}{2}$ per cent on ingots and 50 per cent on cut crystals.
[2] See Appendix for sources of data.

The table indicates that most costs in the above category are of similar magnitude in the two countries, the biggest discrepancy being in rent and building maintenance. These items are less expensive in Israel owing to lower building costs, cheaper labour, and easier weather conditions. The highest item in the table— annual depreciation charges—is, of course, the same in both countries, since the two manufacturing plants use identical equipment. Raw materials consist of reagent grade fine chemicals, which may cost a few dollars per pound. Bearing in mind that a pound of crystals sells for several hundred dollars, raw materials are considered a relatively inexpensive item. Reagent grade lithium fluoride, for example, can be obtained at the price of $13 per kilogram, or about 1 per cent of the sales price of the finished product. The Israeli company will pay a higher price for raw materials as well as for parts and supplies because these items have to be imported.

An additional item—office employment costs—requires some elaboration. These expenses, which are listed in Table V(3), cover the wages of several office workers, who fulfil a somewhat different function in the two countries.

TABLE V(3)

Office and Service Employment

		U.S.	Israel
Manager[1]	$\frac{1}{2}$	$ 9,000	$3,000
Secretary	1	4,000	2,000
Clerk	1	5,000	–
Book-keeper	1	6,000	2,500
		$24,000	$7,500
Fringe benefits		(20%) 4,800	(30%) 2,200
Total office and service employment costs		$28,800	$9,700

The U.S. office, directed by the general manager and staffed by a secretary, clerk, and book-keeper, caters for the needs of both the manufacturing and the marketing departments. The work of the Israeli office is limited to serving the manufacturing end of the firm. It could perhaps do with two instead of three employees, but further reductions are plainly unthinkable, since correspondence

[1] See footnote to Table V(1).

with customers, distributors, and suppliers has to be maintained, accounts must be kept up to date, and shipments have to be packaged and dispatched.

Since the present estimates are concerned with manufacturing costs alone, it is necessary to divide the U.S. office expenses between manufacturing and marketing. Support of the firm's selling efforts requires the bulk of the personnel's time, as will be shown in the next section. Two-thirds of the office employment costs are consequently allocated to marketing, and the remaining $9,600 are included in the estimated manufacturing outlays.

A summary of total outlays (excluding marketing costs) is given in Table V(4), which indicates that the costs of U.S.-made crystals are expected to exceed those of the Israeli exports by over $33,000, or 43 per cent.

The U.S. manufacturer is penalized mainly by high employment costs, which in the present case cannot be counterbalanced by adopting techniques of large-scale manufacture or by exclusive access to external economies. The scale of the operation is

TABLE V(4)

*Summary of Projected Manufacturing and Shipping
Costs of U.S. and Israeli firms*[1]

	(1) U.S.	(2) Israel	(3) ($\frac{2}{1}$) per cent
Manufacturing			
Labour ..	$ 59,400	$23,200	39%
Materials, supplies, and overheads ..	40,900	34,500	86%
Office employment costs ..	9,600*	9,700	101%
Total manufacturing outlays ..	$109,900	$67,400	61%
Shipping ..	—	2,000	
CIF U.S.A. ..	—	$69,400	
Customs duties $10\frac{1}{2}$% ..	—	7,300	
Total landed costs ..	$109,900	$76,700	70%

* These costs are arbitrarily allocated. For details see text
Source: Tables V(1)-V(3).

[1] The table does not take into account internally financed research and development outlays, which are usually small. Since employment costs of scientists account for a major proportion of research and development expenditures in crystals, their inclusion would tend to improve further the cost advantage of the Israeli manufacturer. The bulk of commercial development work is financed by the customers and appears on the profit and loss statement as an operating expense.

restricted by the size and volatility of the market, which does not justify the use of more capital-intensive production methods as in the case of the semiconductor crystals. The existence of university-operated crystals laboratories in Israel provides the local manufacturer with important external economies on terms nearly comparable to those available to his U.S. competitor. The competitive edge of the Israel firm is large enough to absorb the extra shipping costs and customs duties and to leave a substantial margin for covering marketing costs.

The potential cost advantage of the Israel-based manufacturer can be realized, however, only if the rate of plant utilization is similar to that of the U.S. plant. Since many of the cost items are fixed (labour, which accounts for a high proportion of total costs, remains fixed over wide output ranges), average costs are significantly influenced by changes in volume. Unlike his U.S. competitors, the Israeli manufacturer has no sizeable domestic market which can generate the sales volume necessary for a high utilization of his productive capacity. His products must be marketed abroad.

The nature of the marketing function and the magnitude of the costs involved are examined in the next section.

D. MARKET STRUCTURE AND PRACTICES[1]

The U.S. optical crystals market is composed of two distinct sections. Approximately half a million dollars worth of crystals are sold annually to a small number of original equipment manufacturers. Numerous manufacturers of special equipment, research contractors, and laboratories maintained by the armed forces and academic institutions account for an additional $1,000,000 between them. The purchasing practices, fabrication requirements, and pricing methods used in connexion with the two sections are quite dissimilar. It is important to bear the distinctions in mind when considering the marketing practices and problems of the industry.

The purchasing decisions of the original equipment manufacturers and the practices used by them have been largely routinized.

---

[1] The discussion in the present section is based on a detailed survey of the optical crystals market, which constitutes an important segment of the halides crystals market. The other major segment-scintillation crystals-is dealt with explicitly only to the extent that the prevailing marketing practices and problems differ materially between the two segments.

This has been made possible by the fact that the equipment in which crystals are incorporated is being produced to standard specifications which change only slowly from year to year. Four companies control the bulk of the equipment market, in which they compete with each other and with a multitude of small companies. The smaller equipment manufacturers, moreover, usually specify in their routine crystals purchase orders the sizes and shapes used by the major companies. Most of the business conducted in the crystals used by this group may be consequently described as involving fairly standardized products.

Two original equipment manufacturers invite suppliers to bid on the bulk of their requirements, which are usually forecast on an annual basis by the engineering department. The buyers of the other two major equipment makers stated that they rarely request their suppliers to bid. They know from experience which supplier does a better job with a given crystal. The latter is asked to quote a price and delivery dates. The terms of other suppliers can be easily checked if the first does not seem to offer satisfactory service.

University laboratories, commercial development companies, and even manufacturers of special instruments have to specify in detail their crystals requirements practically every time a purchase takes place. The type of the crystals, their shape and their size vary with the type of application, which can seldom be predicted on an annual or semi-annual basis. Consequently, when the need for a crystal becomes apparent, it is the design engineer or the scientist in charge of the project who in fact makes the purchasing decision. Moreover, he is likely to be the person who will decide on the company from which the purchase is going to be made. From past experience he knows which supplier is best qualified to fulfil his needs for a given crystal, and he will instruct the purchasing agent *what* to buy and from *whom* to buy.

The purchasing patterns of this group may be summarized as follows. Total volume per company is small, averaging about $5,000 per annum and varying considerably from company to company. A good part of this total is made up by one or two large and relatively expensive pieces. Windows and random sections[1] make up the remainder. Table V(5), which is based on information supplied by eight small crystal users, illustrates this pattern.

---

[1] Random sections are small chips of crystals used for a variety of purposes where their performance need not conform to close specifications.

TABLE V(5)

Volume and Distribution of Optical Crystals Purchases

Firm No.	Annual Purchase	Size of Minimum Order	Size of Maximum Order
1	$ 3,000	$ 10	$1,000
2	4,500	10	1,400
3	1,000	100	500
4	15,000	50	—
5	3,500	25	—
6	2,000	50	500
7	4,800	400	$1,000
8	9,000	200	500
Range	$1,000–15,000	$10–400	$500–1,400

Another important characteristic of the small users market is the apparent lack of loyalty to a given supplier. The unpredictable changes in the demand patterns are chiefly responsible for this state of affairs. The suppliers, on their part, are unable to adjust their output at very short notice. There is a significant difference between the supply conditions of routine crystals like potassium chloride and calcium fluoride and those of the less frequently used ones. The former are usually stocked by the supplier and are available for delivery either immediately or at short notice. When large quantities are required, the user can usually give ample notice to the supplier, who will schedule his furnaces and work force accordingly. Only small quantities of the less routine crystals are stocked by the manufacturer. The investment seems to be too risky in this case. Thus, when a need for special crystal suddenly arises, the user shops around all available sources of supply. The firm which can deliver the required crystal at the shortest notice usually gets the business, even if its prices are somewhat higher than those of competitors.

Price occupies a prominent place amongst the many elements that enter into the purchasing decision. Its prominence, however, varies with the crystal in question, ranking very highly in the case of standard windows and becoming relatively unimportant when unusual kinds, shapes, or sizes are involved. In the former case demand is standardized and predictable, and several suppliers stand ready to compete for every order. In the latter, demand is erratic: neither the customer nor the supplier is able to predict requirements even a short period ahead.

On the supply side, not every manufacturer has the physical

capacity or the requisite know-how to be able to accept every order coming his way. Moreover, a crystal, even when it is extremely expensive from the manufacturer's point of view, accounts for only a small portion of the cost of the instrument in which it is incorporated. Consequently, the user will frequently be quite prepared to pay a higher price if, in return, he can get improved service in the form of better quality or faster delivery.

The single most important criterion used for establishing prices is volume. Basing prices on volume indeed makes sense, since many of the manufacturing inputs vary with it. Raw materials, electricity consumption, furnace time, and, to some extent, supervision and maintenance change in direct proportion to the size of the crystal. Nevertheless, other elements such as the quantity ordered, shape and dimension, orientation, and other specifications, as well as availability of raw materials and of furnace capacity, affect production costs. Consequently, the basic price of X dollars per c.c. is used as the first approximation for the determination of the final price. The 'other elements' weigh differently with the various manufacturers, who may end up quoting widely divergent prices for a particular order despite the fact that their list prices are similar.

Availability of unused furnace capacity is one of the most important 'other elements'. Since fixed costs account, as was noted above, for a high proportion of total outlays, manufacturers are prepared to grant substantial discounts for large orders which enable them to utilize their equipment more fully. Quantity discounts of 50 per cent or more from the basic price are not uncommon for certain standard crystals.

The telephone is probably the single most important instrument used in negotiations and for placing of orders. A five-minute telephone conversation may accomplish more than an exchange of letters stretching over several weeks. When the crystals user is in a hurry, as he usually is, he will simply not waste his time on correspondence, especially when three or four letters may be required in order to finalize the details of a single transaction. Significantly, phone inquiries to the smaller crystals manufacturers are frequently personally answered by the president.

Salesmen and manufacturers' representatives fulfil only a marginal role in the selling function as it relates to the small users. They cannot hope to cover profitably all the potential customers, who are numerous and have no predictable needs. Moreover, it cannot possibly pay to visit several times a firm which will end up buying $1,000 to $2,000 worth of crystals. Finally, the manufacturer's representative can act at best only as an order taker. He is unlikely to possess the qualifications necessary to discuss all the ramifications involved in the purchase of crystals. Moreover, even if this limitation can be overcome, he must refer all important issues to the head office.

Manufacturers of scintillation crystals on the other hand use the services of manufacturers' representatives to market their crystals. This kind of arrangement seems to pay off where specifications are more standardized. The number of crystals and the varieties of shapes and sizes are more limited in the scintillation field, and the number of users is comparatively small. Consequently potential average sales per customer and per visit are considerably higher than in the case of optical crystals. Under these circumstances, visits to potential customers have a higher probability of paying off, and the salesman or the representative may, indeed, perform an important function. The same considerations apply to the original equipment manufacturers, whose large volume and standardized requirements make them an attractive object of intensive sales efforts. Being small in number, however, they can be cultivated by a senior member of the manufacturer's staff.

A foreign newcomer aspiring to gain a share of the market will obviously be confronted by all the problems faced by his U.S. competitors. In the course of handling these problems he will be handicapped by the fact that his product must be shipped across national borders. He will face other difficulties caused by the physical separation of the manufacturing and marketing arms of his business. These problems are elaborated upon in the next section, which in addition gives estimates of the comparative costs involved in performing the marketing function.

E. THE IMPACT OF ENTRY PROBLEMS ON COMPARATIVE MARKETING COSTS

A foreign crystals supplier seeking entry into the U.S. market must contend with obstacles placed in his way by the Government, with communication difficulties, and with problems of scale.

In addition to imposing a $10\frac{1}{2}$ per cent duty on ingots and 50 per cent on cut and polished crystals, U.S. law, like that of most nations, requires that all goods entering the country should be cleared through customs. This requirement constitutes a nuisance for several reasons. In the first place, it delays the speedy delivery of the goods. Since customs inspection takes place at both the port of departure and the port of arrival, the delay is compounded. A two- or three-day delay in the delivery of crystals is unlikely to prove serious, it is true, since it is customary for crystals to be delivered only several weeks after receipt of the order. The probability of loss or breakage, on the other hand, is definitely enhanced by the necessity of passing customs inspection.

Another Government-made barrier is posed by the so-called 'Buy American' Act. The Act provides that companies should refrain as a rule from using imported goods in connexion with Government-sponsored projects. Only when local products are unavailable, are of inferior quality, or are significantly more expensive than imports is the use of the latter condoned. The vagueness of the Act's provisions, coupled with the fact that crystals pass through numerous stages before being incorporated in an instrument, may help to reduce its impact. It is for instance practically impossible for an equipment purchaser to verify the origin of the components used by his suppliers. The existence of a sizeable non-Government market further reduces the impact of the Act. On the other hand, it is quite likely that crystals users working on Government contract will occasionally refuse to buy foreign-made crystals, regardless of their price and quality, in order to avoid tedious negotiations about relatively unimportant components with unpredictable Government inspectors.

The communication requirements are likely to raise problems of a more serious nature. A major advantage of a local firm is that it has the marketing and manufacturing activities located under the same roof. It was stated above, for example, that the president often handles telephone inquiries personally and that he decides about prices, delivery terms, &c. While answering queries he can consider the schedule of next month's production runs, requirements of a certain raw material, &c. Delivery commitments can therefore be made promptly and on a firm basis.

Proximity to the fabricating plant enables the U.S. manufacturer to test the cleaving characteristics of a crystal from a new run before completing it. The availability of testing services in a nearby town allows him to measure without delay the characteristics of a crystal about which he has doubts, or to check the complaints of a dissatisfied customer. He may send a sample to the customer for his examination before proceeding with another batch, and so on. Such flexibility will, of course, be denied to the foreign manufacturer. The home office has to be consulted before important commitments to the customers can be made, and crystals cannot be shuttled back and forth between Israel and the U.S. for testing and checking.

The marketing, just like the manufacturing, function may, in short, benefit from external economies. These economies are available, however, only to the local manufacturer, whose lines of communication are short and who can act without undue delay upon feedback received from the market. The fact that the same person directs in most cases both the manufacturing and marketing activities automatically provides for effective communication channels between the two functions. The risks of mistakes and misunderstandings are similarly reduced, and the chances of taking immediate remedial action, when necessary, are enhanced.

The necessity of dividing the chief executive's job between two people penalizes the exporter in an additional, and more tangible, sense: when two persons do the job which is performed by only one person in the domestic firm, neither is fully utilized, and costly duplication is unavoidable. Each of these executives represents, like a piece of large and specialized equipment, an indivisible investment which cannot be obtained in smaller units. Without having the services of a qualified marketing man who has a thorough knowledge of the crystals field, the exporter is unlikely to sell his output. Yet the talents of this man are only partly utilized, because of the limited sales volume he handles on the one hand and his physical separation from the manufacturing facility on the other. The same applies of course to the manufacturing manager who is directing only a small-scale operation, and to the staff which assists these executives.

In summary, a price of reduced efficiency, costly communications, and duplication of executive and service functions has to be paid for the maintenance of physically separated manufacturing and marketing organizations. An estimate of the costs involved is given in Table V(6), which compares the marketing outlays of the exporter and the local manufacturer.

TABLE V(6)

Comparative Marketing Costs

Employment Costs			U.S.	Israel
Sales manager	1	..		$18,000
Secretary	1	..		4,000
Shipping clerk	1	..		5,000
Crystals cutter	1	..		7,000
				$34,000
Fringe benefits 20%				6,800
U.S. expenses—⅔ of the office costs listed in Table V(3)		..	$19,200	———
			$19,200	$40,800

Office and Sales Expenses				
Participation in exhibitions	..		$ 3,000	$ 3,000
Catalogue and other promotion	..		3,500	3,500
Shipping and postage	..		500	500
Telephone	..		3,600	4,200
Rent and maintenance	..		4,000	8,000
Professional services	..		1,500	1,000
Miscellaneous	..		1,000	1,000
Travel	..		1,000	4,000
Total office and sales expenses	..		$18,100	$25,200
Total marketing costs	..		$37,300	$66,000

The Israeli exporter is assumed to maintain a sales office in the U.S. which is staffed by three persons, in addition to the manager. Their employment costs amount to $40,800. The local manufacturer's office employment costs were given in Table V(3). Two-thirds of these costs, or $19,200, are assumed to be spent in support of the marketing function.

Several individual cost items require comments. Note, for example, that the exporter employs a crystals cutter at the cost of $7,000 per annum. It will be recalled that U.S.-made crystals are cut by the manufacturing department as part of its routine functions. The exporter is prevented from following this sensible expedient because of the U.S. customs duties, which rise to 50 per cent in the case of cut or polished crystals. The lower rent of the U.S. firm is explained by the fact that all its departments are housed under one roof. The exporter will have to rent separate facilities for the marketing department. He will also incur heavy travelling expenses, which cannot be avoided if face-to-face communication between marketing and production executives is to be maintained.

Table V(7) summarizes the cost components discussed above, and puts into focus the differences in the operating structure of the two firms.

TABLE V(7)

Summary of Total Outlays—U.S. and Israeli
Crystals Operations

	(1) U.S.	(2) Israel	(3) $\frac{2}{1}$%
Manufacturing (a)			
Labour ..	$ 59,400	$ 23,200	39
Materials supplies and overheads			
incl. office employment costs ..	50,500	44,200	87
Total manufacturing ..	109,900	67,400	61
Shipping and customs duties ..	—	9,300	—
Marketing (b) ..	37,300	66,000	177
Total costs ..	$147,200	$142,700	97

Source: (a) Table V(4)   (b) Table V(6).

The table shows clearly that the Israel-based plant can produce crystals at costs representing substantial savings over those incurred by the U.S. competition. The figures are equally clear about the relative disadvantage which the Israeli exporter suffers in the marketing area, where his costs exceed those of the U.S. competitor by nearly 80 per cent. Total costs are $142,700 for imported versus $147,200 for U.S.-made crystals. The difference of less than $5,000, or 3 per cent, is hardly significant, considering the tentative nature and crudeness of the estimates, and considering further that financial charges, which are likely to be considerably higher in Israel, were not included in the calculations.

The above conclusions might be objected to on the grounds that they pertain only to a particular case which has no general validity. Moreover, it might be argued that even in the present case several cost-cutting avenues are open to the exporter. He might, for example, cut his costs by simply handing the selling function over to a specialized distributor. Since the latter handles as a rule the products of several manufacturers, he may achieve the economies of scale denied to the exporter, doing his own marketing.

Scintillation crystals, and standard optical crystals of the kind used by manufacturers of original equipment, may indeed be handled in that fashion. The manufacturer's representative, however, cannot act as much more than a contact man and an order taker who refers the less routine matters back to head office. A competent representative of head office must consequently be located near the major customers in order to be in a position to take up the contacts developed by the representative. The scant use made of representatives by optical crystals manufacturers suggests that this method of selling is inappropriate for non-routine crystals and in general for specialized or custom-made products.

It could be argued that the exporter has another alternative. He could attain a higher utilization of his capacity by simply expanding sales. Higher output, however, is ruled out by the assumptions stated at the beginning of the chapter. In view of the fact that the optical crystals market does not exceed $1,500,000, it is unlikely that a foreign entrant could hope to control a higher share without provoking the local manufacturers into costly price wars based on marginal cost pricing and demands for Government protection.[1] A small market is a characteristic which, by the definition of the present study, is common to first-phase industries. The sales volume of other first-phase products is consequently likely to be of an order of magnitude similar to that of the various segments of the crystals market. The problem of excess capacity can under these circumstances be satisfactorily solved only by firms in which the managerial functions are performed by a minimum number of persons.

Is the exporter better placed in regard to custom-made products whose unit value is relatively high? A producer of high-priced equipment used in space exploration, for example, may operate on a large enough scale to require that the marketing and manufacturing functions be managed by different persons. Yet, if the firm is located far from its major customers, it may have to duplicate its

---

[1] Since the Government is an important customer it can discriminate against foreign suppliers by interpreting the provisions of the 'Buy American' Act in a strict manner. Thus local industry may gain from additional protection without increase in import duties.

testing or research facilities in order to be able to service them properly. In addition it appears that the manufacture of unique, high-priced products requires close and continuous face-to-face communication between the manufacturer and his customers, suppliers, and subcontractors. The New York regional study mentioned earlier amply illustrates how manufacturers of first-phase products congregate in close proximity to one another and to the market, in order to benefit from common services and to minimize communication problems.

Several general conclusions regarding the factors which determine the competitive potential which Israel has in first-phase products emerge from the above discussion. Israel (and countries having a similar economic structure) has a substantial cost advantage in professional labour and a smaller one in unskilled labour. Against this, it suffers from a distinct disadvantage in marketing though this disadvantage is confined to export products. Since, however, the country has practically no internal market for sophisticated first-phase products, local manufacturers must contend with the difficulties involved in marketing their output abroad.

Competitors located in the U.S. benefit from an additional advantage, owing to their ready access to external economies. Unlike labour and raw materials, external economies are not a tangible production factor which can be directly measured. Indirectly, however, this factor is represented by the relative cost of supplies, materials, freight, and services rendered by subcontractors. In the case considered here external economies did not figure prominently in the production costs, since both the U.S. and the Israeli plant were shown to have little use for external services, while having ready access to information and advice available from academic institutions involved in research and development work.

By contrast, the importance of both internal and external economies in marketing was shown to be considerable. Proximity to the market enables U.S. manufacturers to minimize their overheads and to maintain effective communications between the marketing and production departments on the one hand and the customers on the other.

The findings reported in this chapter are not too significant in the statistical sense, because of the limited scope of the empirical observations, and because of the nature of the cost data, which were based on hypothetical rather than on actual figures. Additional research into the nature and structure of several other products is necessary before these findings can be regarded as conclusive. At the same time it is highly likely that additional research will indicate that even if Israel and similar countries can be shown to have a competitive potential in the *manufacture* of new products, this potential cannot be readily translated into exports because of the marketing problems and high export marketing costs. Some measures which might be adopted to offset these adverse effects are considered in the next chapter, which is concerned with the normative conclusions suggested by the discussion of chapters one to five.

Appendix: Sources of Data and Methodology Used in Chapter V

The material presented in Chapter V is based on a market study prepared by the writer for Prototech Incorporated, a subsidiary of Bolt Beranek and Newman, Cambridge, Mass., during the summer of 1964. It became apparent at the outset of the inquiry that there is practically no published literature on the economic aspects of the crystals field and that the established manufacturers are generally secretive and reluctant to reveal any meaningful information about their operations. The bulk of the information was consequently gathered from crystals users and scientists involved in crystal growing in non-commercial institutions such as university laboratories.

Personal interviews were conducted with several of the largest optical instruments manufacturers. Additional information was obtained by means of a questionnaire which was mailed to about 250 companies in the infra-red, ultra-violet, radiation detection, and laser instruments business. Replies were received from thirty-two companies, fifteen of which turned out to be crystals users. While there is reason to believe that the response to the questionnaire was definitely non-representative of the 'industry' as a whole, the data obtained from these responses were both informative and valuable. The methods used to arrive at specific estimates and the sources of the data on which they are based are discussed below.

Output volume and furnace requirements

Output volume depends on a number of variables, including the number of furnaces and their size, the growing rate, and yield.

Yield refers simply to the ratio of successful crystals grown. The skills of the grower in controlling the temperatures and in preparing the raw material affect the yield, which, in addition, may vary with the rigidity of the specifications. For very tough specifications, it is likely that only 50 or 60 per cent of the crystals grown will be usable. For the more run-of-the-mill crystals, where the specifications are not too rigid, a higher yield, approaching 100 per cent in certain cases, may be expected.

The term 'yield' may be viewed in two different ways. A run may yield a 70 per cent output in the sense that only parts of the crystal grown are usable commercially. The remaining parts are cut out, reground, and used over again as raw material. A large crystal typically yields materials of different quality ranging from excellent to outright useless. A 70 per cent yield may also be viewed in a different sense. Out of ten crystals grown, seven runs are successful and the remainder are not up to specifications. This approach applies to experimental crystals and generally to crystals which have to be grown to rigid specifications. When uniform doping or exact orientation is important, a crystal is either usable or useless. The last statement should be somewhat qualified, since a crystal which is of no value to 'A' may still be of interest to 'B', though possibly only at a reduced price. In summary, yield in the present context is an economic rather than a mechanical concept. This distinction is important in connexion with the determination of the furnace and manpower requirements of the plant.

The method of calculating furnace requirements deserves a detailed discussion, since it takes into account yield, cycle time, product mix, and several other economic and technical aspects of crystal growing which should be clarified. Table V(8) illustrates the calculating procedure used and how the variables mentioned above affect the number of required furnaces.

Assuming that the plant is going to produce medium-size, medium-priced crystals of 150 mm. diameter by 100 mm. thickness, the number of requisite furnaces may then be calculated as follows: (1) Calculate dollar receipts per run. This can be done by first calculating the volume per crystal in cubic cm. and by multiplying the volume by price per cm.^{3}—$2.50. The resulting figure is then multiplied by the yield, which in the case on hand was assumed to vary between 70 and 85 per cent. (2) The required number of runs per year is next calculated by dividing the receipts

TABLE V(8)

*Calculation of Furnace Requirements for a Firm
Specializing in Medium-Sized, Medium-Priced
Crystals*

Line	Method of Calculation			
1	Dimension—up to 50 mm. dia. × 75 mm. thick			
2	Volume: gross—up to 147 cm.^{3}			
3	Price (a) $2.5/cm.^{3}			
4	Yield per run	70%	80%	85%
5	Volume net (2) × (4)	103 cm.^{3}	118 cm.^{3}	125 cm.^{3}
6	Receipts per run (5) × (3)	$258	$295	$313
7	Required runs per year $200,000 divided by (6)	78	68	64
8	Available weeks per year		48	
9	Cycle time—weeks per run (b)		4	
10	Runs per year (8) divided by (9)		12	
11	Required number of furnaces (7) divided by (10)	7	6	6

(a) Average list price of three U.S. companies for lithium fluoride and magnesium fluoride crystals.

(b) Estimate given by scientists from the crystal-growing laboratories of M.I.T. and Lincoln Laboratories.

per run into 200,000, the annual sales estimate. This figure, of course, varies with the yield, ranging in the example from 78 for a yield of 70 per cent, to 64 for an 85 per cent yield.

Next, it is necessary to find out how many crystals can be grown over the year. This is done by dividing 'cycle time', measured here in weeks, into the number of available weeks per year. The 'available weeks per year' are calculated by deducting from 52 a given number of weeks which are necessary for repair work, overhaul, plant shutdown, and other contingencies. In this case, it was assumed that 48 weeks a year are available for production. Available information suggests that crystals of the volume indicated above take about 4 weeks to grow. Dividing 4 into 48 gives a total of 12 runs per year. The number of required furnaces is finally arrived at by dividing this figure into the number of annual runs. The table shows that the number of furnaces will vary between 7, if 78 runs per year are required, and 6, if only 64 runs are necessary.

Sources of other data

Wages: U.S.—Controller's department of Bolt Beranek and Newman.

Israel—State of Israel Investment Authority, *Investors' Manual No. 8; Labor Relations and Wages* (Jerusalem, 1962). Costs were adjusted for subsequent wage rises.

Raw Materials: the price lists of several chemical supply houses which supply reagent grade fluorides used for crystal growing average around $13 per kilogram. Assuming an additional $0.5 per kilogram for freight to Israel, raw material costs for both plants are calculated as follows:

	U.S.	Israel
Annual requirements[1]	200 kg.	200 kg.
Price	$13/kg.	$13.50/kg.
Cost of raw materials	$2,600	$2,700

Electricity: annual consumption was estimated at about 150,000 kWh. on the basis of information obtained from the crystal-growing operations of M.I.T. and Lincoln Laboratories. An executive of the Cambridge Electric Company estimated the lowest industrial rates available in Massachusetts at 1.5 cents per kWh. An Israel Government publication quotes industrial rates at about 1.2 cents per kWh.[2]

It should be noted in this connexion that despite the lower price prevailing in Israel, electricity there is regarded as a high-cost input. This seeming paradox can be resolved simply: electricity is indeed an expensive input in Israel when its cost is compared to that of labour. The ratio of U.S. to Israel labour costs is about 2.5 to 1, whereas the ratio of electricity costs is closer to unity.

Depreciation: identical depreciation rates of $15,000 per year were calculated for both plants. This figure assumes an investment in furnaces and auxiliary equipment totalling $150,000. Estimates of the outlays for capital equipment were obtained from M.I.T. crystal-growing laboratory, the Arthur D. Little Company of Cambridge, Mass., and the crystal-growing laboratory of the Hebrew University, Jerusalem. Higher freight charges payable on imported equipment in Israel are offset by the lower cost of locally produced equipment.

[1] Annual requirements are calculated by dividing the physical volume (see Table V(8)) by the specific weight of the chemical compound.

[2] State of Israel Investment Authority, *Investors' Manual No. 10; Electricity Fuel and Water* (Jerusalem, G.P.O., 1963).

Rent and Maintenance: the estimates are based on the following assumptions:

	U.S.	Israel
Space required (sq. feet)	4,000	4,000
Rent and maintenance per sq. foot	$3	$1.25
Cost of rent and maintenance	12,000	5,000

U.S. costs were estimated on the basis of the experience of Bolt Beranek and Newman. Estimated outlays in Israel are based on the assumption that the differential in the cost of rent and maintenance between the two countries is of the same order of magnitude as the difference between average labour rates. The lower costs in Israel are attributable to cheaper labour and easy weather conditions which allow for light construction and low heating charges.

Freight: it is assumed that crystals will be shipped by air, using the Post Office as carrier. Rates quoted by the U.S. Post Office are about $6 per kilogram. Shipping costs for 200 kilograms are $1,200. $800 were added to this sum to account for insurance and packaging.

The remaining costs estimates, including sales promotion, office rent, professional services, &c., are based on figures provided by the controller of Bolt Beranek and Newman.

VI

POLICIES FOR EXPORT PROMOTION

A. INTRODUCTION

THE introduction to this study stated that one of its aims was to develop and test a model which might be useful for . . . 'formulating policies designed to bridge the gap between the competitive potential of different industries and their actual export performance'.[1] This concluding chapter is concerned with the normative implications which follow from the verification of the major premises of the product-cycle model.

The model indicates that the stage of economic development reached by a country is a major determinant of the kind and characteristics of the products in which it can expect to have a competitive advantage. It suggest further that the problems of gaining access to foreign markets vary in a systematic fashion with the characteristics of the products which a country seeks to export.

Chapter II distinguished between three types of economies whose structure and factor endowment set them apart from each other: (1) The less developed economies ('L' countries), which include countries such as Argentina, India, Turkey, and Hong Kong, countries where 'the first stages of industrialization have been completed';[2] (2) The small and developed economies ('D' countries: Holland, Switzerland, Denmark, and (in certain respects) Israel are included in this group)[3]; (3) The industrial

---

[1] Chapter I, p. 1.

[2] A. K. Caincross, *Factors in Economic Development* (London, George Allen and Unwin Ltd., 1962), p. 206. Countries which are just beginning to industrialize are not considered in the study.

[3] Those readers, who like the writer, have some doubt about the propriety of considering Israel as a developed country might take note of the following paragraph which compares Israel to Denmark:

'A small country to which Israel might look for an example of what can be done in electronic manufacturing is Denmark. Denmark has a well-developed professional-equipment industry, as is recommended for Israel; has a high percentage of export, as is desired by Israel, and with a population of 4.5 million as

leaders ('A' countries), which are headed by the U.S. Other countries which may be regarded as belonging to this group are Germany, Great Britain, and France.[1]

The 'L' countries have a lower per capita income and a narrow industrial base which lacks technological sophistication. Their economies are characterized by scarcity of capital, engineers, scientists, administration, and external economies. Unskilled labour is the one economic input which is in abundant supply, apart from exploitable natural resources, whose availability is independent of an economy's stage of development.[2] Many of the more sophisticated industrial products are obtained by the 'L' countries abroad. Their exports consist mainly of industrial raw materials, semi-manufactured goods, and agricultural commodities.

By comparison, the small developed countries have a high average income, a diversified industrial base, and an adequate supply of engineering and scientific talents. Because of their small size, the 'D' countries have a large stake in foreign trade. Imports supply a large proportion of their needs, and exports absorb a substantial part of their available resources.

The industrial leaders are, as the title implies, richly supplied with capital, skills, and external economies, which enable them to maintain a wide industrial base and a high average income level. They are less dependent on foreign trade than the other two groups, because of the large size of their markets, the abundance of economic resources, and the variety of products which they are able to produce competitively.

The next section discusses, first, the characteristics of the products

---

compared with Israel's 2.5 million; Israel, (even with a smaller population) produces approximately the same number of electronic engineers as Denmark does,'

Stanford Research Institute, *A Study of the Potential For the Development of an Electronics Industry in Israel* (Menlo Park, 1962), p. 6.

The above supports the claim that Israel is at least approaching the status of a developed country. The problems it encounters in developing an electronics industry are likely to be indicative of those faced by other, more developed countries having a similar economic structure, even if the other countries are more advanced in most respects.

[1] The smaller members of the E.E.C. might be considered as 'candidates' for the last group. They will become 'full members' once the E.E.C. realizes its goals and becomes a true economic union.

[2] Some 'L' countries have mineral deposits and other sources of raw materials whereas others lack them. Natural resources are therefore not considered here as an input which all 'L' countries have.

in which countries belonging to the three economic groups have a competitive potential, and secondly, the issues confronting policy-makers concerned with the realization of this potential.

B. THE LESS DEVELOPED COUNTRIES

The product-cycle model indicates that the less developed countries can expect to have a competitive advantage in mature products. The production process of these products is usually stable and is suitable for long runs of uniform output. Consequently, unskilled and semi-skilled workers, whose employment costs are low, make up the bulk of the labour force. The need for scarce scientists and engineers, on the other hand, is comparatively limited.

Mature products have one undesirable attribute, however: they tend to have a comparatively high capital content. Capital costs in developing countries are rather high, and the utilization of capital-intensive production processes will undoubtedly raise manufacturing costs. The adverse effects of the higher capital charges may, however, be offset by the fact that the employment of other scarce inputs can be minimized. The limited need of mature industries for scientists and engineers, their relative independence of external economies, and their adaptability to imported technologies allow the developing countries to economize on resources which may be even scarcer than capital.

The standardized nature of mature products facilitates easy communication between the exporters and the market. Steel, bulk chemicals, certain types of cloth, other commodities, and standardized manufactures can be bought throughout the world on the basis of universally accepted specifications regarding shapes, sizes, quality, and price. It is possible, for example, for a steel merchant located in Africa to inform his British suppliers of his exact requirements by stating the specifications of the goods he needs in simple terms which are fully understood by both parties. Frequent face-to-face communications are not needed, and the chances of misunderstandings are comparatively remote.

While the communication problems involving standardized consumer products or industrial components are somewhat more complicated, they may still be handled with relative ease. A Japanese radio manufacturer has little difficulty in ascertaining the shape, colour, and performance characteristics of transistor radios which are popular in the U.S. His distributors or agents can convey their exact requirements by sending to him a few relatively simple engineering drawings and component specifications which have the same meaning in Japan as in the U.S.

The ease with which information on mature products can be communicated back and forth between the manufacturer and the market reduces the marketing costs of these products and enhances their 'export worthiness'. This fact has particular significance for manufacturers located in the developing countries. The products which they sell in the domestic markets are either not suitable for export at all, or else only with considerable modification. It is unlikely, for example, that household appliances, clothes, entertainment equipment, and other consumer goods enjoying popularity in India, Colombia, or even Japan will find a ready market in the U.S. Differences in tastes, styles, and acceptable price ranges between countries having such different income levels and cultural traits are likely to be considerable. The same considerations apply to industrial goods. It is hardly conceivable that U.S. manufacturers will have widespread use for equipment and components designed and produced by manufacturers in the developing countries to satisfy primarily the needs of their own *domestic markets*. Products sold to the advanced countries must consequently be specifically designed and manufactured for export.

Failure to adjust one's specifications to the exact requirements of the customers may cost the exporter dearly as the following example shows:

Most Rhodesians like to keep on hand bottles of drinks and these must be stored in the refrigerator. It has been suggested that on more than one occasion the U.K. lost ground on this market simply because their refrigerators did not take into account of the need for storing a considerably larger number of bottles than was the case in Great Britain.

Another example explains why British exporters of washing machines lost ground in Rhodesia:

Demand for washing machines in the Federation rose between 1953 and 1959. But since these machines were operated mainly by African servants, and consequently were apt to be somewhat roughly treated, toughness was of greater importance than the proliferation of labor-saving gadgets of the machines. Hot water was usually readily available from kitchen heaters and the heating element in the machine was therefore regarded as something of a luxury.[1]

The difficulties involved in obtaining the information which could lead to *altering* the appliances made in Britain to suit the needs of the Rhodesians are surely minute in comparison with the problems encountered by manufacturers in developing countries who have to rely on feedback from distant markets to guide their *entire* manufacturing activities.

The competitive potential which developing countries have in mature goods is further enhanced by the fact that selling problems are comparatively simple owing to the nature of the products and of the demand for them. The price range within which mature products of a given quality and performance characteristics can be sold is comparatively narrow and easily ascertained. Buyers are price-conscious, and are on the lookout for less expensive supplies. Exporters from developing countries can consequently gain access to foreign markets by offering their goods at competitive prices.

The selling job of the exporters is likely to be further simplified by the fact that markets for commodities, non-differentiated manufactures, and standardized manufactures tend to be highly organized. Auctions and bidding are means which are commonly used to bring buyers and sellers together. Even when sales have to be individually negotiated, all parties to the transaction are, as a rule, well informed of the relevant market facts such as prevailing prices and supply conditions.

Empirical evidence discussed in Chapter IV supported, on the whole, the premises of the model. The chapter showed that the competitive position of the U.S. electronics industry was strongest in the labour-intensive Government and industrial products sector and weakest in the capital-intensive consumer goods. The U.S. imports these goods in considerable volume from Japan and Hong Kong.

These findings conflict with the oft-repeated assertion that these countries managed to establish their competitive position mainly because of their low labour costs. If this were the case, Japan's comparative advantage would lie in the labour-intensive products and not in the mass-produced, capital-intensive, consumer goods.

---

[1] S. Wells, *British Export Performance—A Comparative Study* (Cambridge University Press, 1964), p. 152.

Mr. Robert Sprague, who pleaded the case of the U.S. electronics industry before the Federal Tariff Commission, probably came closer to identifying the nature of the foreign manufacturers' strength when he described their products as having 'a standardized high volume market here which gives these items the market aspects of basic commodities . . .'.[1]

The remarkable performance of the Hong Kong electronics industry indicates that the horizons of exporters from less developed countries need not be limited to textiles and other traditional commodities, provided they are willing to assume the risks involved in marketing more differentiated products abroad.

Lacking space and natural resources, the four million inhabitants of this tiny colony are forced to devote an unusually high proportion of their economic activities to foreign trade. 'Roughly 90 per cent of Hong Kong's production is exported, while it relies on imports for three-quarters of its food supply and all raw materials except sand and building stone.'[2]

The colony's major industrial activities were traditionally, and are still, centred on the textile industry, which in 1964 employed 40 per cent of the recorded industrial labour force.[3] Pressures from the domestic textile industries in the U.S. and Britain, the colony's major trading partners, led to negotiations which culminated in the imposition of 'voluntary' quotas restricting the future expansion of textile exports to the West. Increasing obstacles were also placed in the way of the Hong Kong textile exporters in the markets of several developing countries where recently established local firms, aided by Government regulation of imports, have been gradually displacing foreign suppliers. Faced with growing restrictions on their traditional exports, Hong Kong's businessmen turned their attention to other fields of endeavour, and consequently:

The electronics industry has experienced an explosive growth spurred by the production of small transistor radios. Starting with but one factory assembling radio sets from imported parts late in 1959, there are now

[1] Statement of Robert C. Sprague, appearing as Chairman of the Electronic Imports Committee of the Electronic Industries Association before the U.S. Tariff Commission and the Trade Information Committee, 10 March 1964; mimeographed speech, p. 17.
[2] First National City Bank, *Foreign Information Service* Hong Kong (New York, 8 January, 1965), p. 8.
[3] Ibid., p. 5.

about 25 active in the field. An increasing share of components is locally made and annual output is now approaching four million radios.[1]

The experience of Hong Kong indicates that if the Governments of the less developed countries wish to induce local businessmen to establish modern export industries, they should recreate the conditions which brought the Hong Kong electronics industry into being.

It is of course impossible to say for sure whether the industry would have been developed at all, or at any rate so rapidly, if Hong Kong's traditional exports had not been threatened by external forces which, by their very nature, were beyond the control of the exporters. The absence of relatively modern industries in numerous developing countries more generously endowed with space and economic resources than Hong Kong is, however, significant in this respect. It implies that strong inducements are necessary to divert capital and labour from their employment in the traditional fields.

The colony's businessmen and workers could hardly be expected to welcome the curbs imposed on their traditional exports. They would have undoubtedly preferred to continue expanding the textile industry upon which their prosperity and reputation were founded. Foreign countries, however, could not be coerced into purchasing goods which they did not want, and Hong Kong's businessmen were forced to develop new products which were acceptable abroad.

Hong Kong's industrialists responded to adverse developments in foreign textile markets because they had no choice. The dependence of the economy on foreign trade is so acute that failure to react to changes in the conditions prevailing abroad would have undoubtedly hit hard a large number of businesses, and would have had noticeable repercussions throughout the economy.

The export sector of most countries is smaller than in Hong Kong, and most businessmen find sufficient scope in the local markets. Discussing the conditions faced by the average businessman in the developing countries, R. Vernon states that 'At home, such entrepreneurs often confront a market characterized by suppressed demand, extensive restrictions, and limited domestic competition. There may be risks; but the risks are much less on the demand side than on the supply side. . . . When selling in world markets, on the other hand, the risks on the demand side tend to be of another order of magnitude. . . .'[1] The author deals in the article in detail with the risks confronting exporters in the less developed countries, and he shows that failure to enter the export business, given the opportunities at home, is based on rational evaluation of the risks and prospects in both markets. In order to widen the circle of potential exporters, it may be necessary to establish domestic economic conditions which oblige businessmen to seek export markets for their products in order to avoid losses or even bankruptcy.

Israel's textile and clothing industry provides an example of how such a policy can be made to work. In an effort to force the industry to improve efficiency and to increase exports, the Government embarked in 1955 upon a massive investment programme designed to expand productive capacity well beyond the needs of the domestic market.

Government loans of twenty-six million Israel pounds were granted to a large number of textile firms during the period 1955-8.[2] These loans accounted for 20 per cent of the total capital advanced by the Government to industry during these years. Few manufacturers, small or large, could afford to turn down the offers of cheap loans for expansion. Failure to expand when other plants in the industry increased their capacity implied that the enterprise would be unable to compete with the modern up-to-date plants whose expansion enabled them to reduce unit costs by increasing the scale of their operations.

Larger output was accompanied, as was anticipated, by sharp increases in exports. Production and trade statistics indicate that the policy of the Government was effective. Exports of textiles and clothing rose from $5.8 million to $31.1 million during the 1956-62 period, an increase of over 530 per cent. Total output of the textile industry during the period increased by less than 300 per cent.[3]

The wisdom of the Government's policy might be questioned on the grounds that the mature textile industry should not have been allocated scarce labour, capital, and management resources

---

[1] R. Vernon, 'Problems and prospects in the Export of Manufactured Goods from the Less-Developed Countries', U.N. Conference on Trade and Development, Contributed Paper (New York, December 1963).

[2] Ministry of Commerce and Industry, *Israel's Industrial Future 1960-1965* (Jerusalem, Government Printing Office, 1960).

[3] Ministry of Commerce and Industry, *Program for Israel's Industrial Development—A Second Look 1965-1970* (Jerusalem, G.P.O., 1964), p. 233.

which might have been more effectively utilized in more modern industries. The experience of the textile industry in Israel shows, however, that a policy of deliberately increasing the capacity of an industry beyond the requirements of the local market may help to reduce unit costs and to increase exports.

In summary, developing countries can expect to employ their inexpensive labour supply to best advantage in mature industries whose technology and output volume have reached comparative stability. Choice of such industries enables them to trade off scarce external economies, management talents, and scientific inputs against higher capital charges and to economize on their scarcest resources. By choosing products sold in well-organized, price-sensitive markets, they can reduce marketing costs and minimize the risks caused by their dependence on foreign markets.

C. THE INDUSTRIAL LEADERS

The industrial leaders (the 'A' countries) are abundantly endowed with all factors of production. Skilled labour, engineering, scientific, and management talents as well as external economies and capital are available to local manufacturers in ample quantities. Technically, the 'A' countries are capable of manufacturing most new (first-phase), growth (second-phase), and mature (third-phase) products. It is quite likely, moreover, that the U.S. for example has an *absolute* advantage in many of the products which it actually imports. The product-cycle model suggests that the 'A' countries' *comparative* advantage is in second-phase products, because some of the inputs which are important in the manufacture of these products are abundant in the 'A' countries and scarce in the 'L' and 'D' countries.

Chapter IV indicated, in agreement with the model, that the U.S. electronics industry has a strong international position in growth products whose sales volume is expanding at a high rate. These products were shown to have a high labour and skill content, and their capital content is comparatively low. The competitive position of the U.S. in mass-produced electronic consumer products was shown, by contrast, to be weakening. These products, which have reached the mature stage in the U.S., are capital-intensive, and their skill content is comparatively low.

The industrial leaders may also have a competitive edge in certain mature products which have a particularly high capital content, since capital, as was noted above, is scarce in the less developed economies. Certain chemicals, the automotive industry and electrical machinery are cases in point. Similarly, the 'A' countries are likely to be competitive in first-phase products with a high capital component, and in those whose manufacture depends on extensive utilization of external economies. Computers, aircraft embodying new technologies, and atomic reactors are examples which come immediately to mind.

In summary, the industrial leaders enjoy a competitive advantage in growth products because they have ample supplies of the capital, skills, external economies, and management talent which are intensively utilized in the manufacture of these products. The abundance of these production factors also enables them to compete in those mature products which are highly capital-intensive, and in new products which depend on extensive external economies. Moreover, the differential between local and export marketing costs protects domestic manufacturers of first-phase products against competitive imports of such products.

D. THE SMALL DEVELOPED COUNTRIES

Despite the many dissimilarities, the less developed countries and the small developed countries have several characteristics in common. Both have small internal markets and limited external economies, and both depend on imports to supply a substantial proportion of their economic resources.[1] To improve their trade balance, neither can rely on an indefinite expansion of traditional exports. Consequently, in order to increase their foreign exchange earnings, they must develop export-oriented industries which are relatively advanced technologically (in terms of the existing industries which cater for the home market).

The product-cycle model indicates that the 'D' countries have a competitive potential in new products which are going through the first phase of the product cycle. First-phase products contain a high proportion of scientific and engineering inputs, which are

[1] S. Kuznets, *Six Lectures on Economic Growth* (Glencoe, Ill. The Free Press, 1939).

comparatively abundant in the 'D' countries. They are less likely to be competitive in mature products, because their labour costs are higher than in the less developed economies and capital is more expensive than in the countries here designated as industrial leaders or 'A' countries.

The small array of external economies available to manufacturers in the 'D' countries limits the range of new products which can be manufactured domestically on a competitive basis. The list of exportable products is further reduced by the necessity to maintain frequent face-to-face communications with the customers, to obtain from them product specifications, and to provide them with extensive post-sale services. The manufacturer must often establish a separate marketing organization abroad so as to be in a position to fulfil these functions effectively. The costs involved are high and usually exceed those incurred by the domestic competitors by a large margin. It was shown in Chapter V, for example, that the marketing costs of an Israeli crystals manufacturer are likely to be considerably higher than those of a U.S.-based manufacturer. Moreover, estimated marketing outlays of the former were shown to account for a high proportion of total costs, exceeding manufacturing costs by several percentage points.

The risks involved in exporting new products abroad are increased in several respects when domestic markets for these prodducts are small or non-existent.

Equipment, materials, labour, and management time must be committed to export projects. In addition, substantial investments must be made, as was shown above, in the creation of an efficient marketing organization abroad. The resources thus committed are not likely to be transferable to alternative uses without difficulties and financial sacrifices, owing to the dissimilarities between the characteristics of the products manufactured for export on the one hand and for the local markets on the other. Under these conditions, exporting cannot be treated as a marginal activity which can pay for itself by covering incremental costs. Unless prospects of generating sufficient earnings to recover fully the total investments made in export projects are favourable, businessmen are unlikely to undertake such investments.

The specialized nature of the export products may, moreover, make economies of scale difficult to attain. If plant and equipment used to manufacture export products can only be used for the purpose of serving foreign markets, a comparatively high sales volume must be expected with some confidence before such an investment is justified. If less specialized equipment is installed to minimize the risks involved in wide sales fluctuations or loss of foreign markets, unit production costs are likely to be high.

To be competitive, manufacturers of the 'D' countries might concentrate on a limited range of new products which are least affected by the adverse factors discussed above. They should select products containing comparatively high scientific and engineering inputs to maximize the utilization of production factors in which the 'D' countries have their most substantial advantage. The use of capital and of unskilled labour, which are comparatively expensive, should, on the other hand, be limited as far as possible.

Marketing costs of exporters of new products were shown to be substantially higher than those incurred by local suppliers. To minimize this disadvantage, exporters should select products whose marketing costs account for as low a percentage of total costs as possible. Similarly, these products should not require extensive post-selling servicing by the manufacturers, since the costs involved in this are likely to be prohibitive.

Since external economies are scarce in the 'D' countries, manufacturers should select products whose manufacture is as independent of external economies as possible. At the same time they should make maximum use of the testing facilities, professional expertise, and ancillary services which can be provided by local scientific institutions, professional organizations, and existing industries. It was noted in Chapter V, for example, that the availability of crystal-growing facilities in scientific institutions might provide a necessary (though by no means a sufficient) basis for the establishment in Israel of an export-oriented crystal-growing enterprise. If the Israeli manufacturer discussed in Chapter V has to depend on the U.S. for laboratory services and specifications, he could not possibly expect to compete with U.S. manufacturers.

It might be interesting, in this respect, to note the recommendations contained in a report dealing with the prospects of the Israel electronics industry which was prepared by a team of experts from the Stanford Research Institute. The report recommended that the Israel industry should concentrate on eight product lines.[1] Two product lines, teaching devices and medical devices, deserve particular note because of the reasons given by the authors of the report for their inclusion:

> For medical equipment, Israel's strong position in the world of medical research, high density of doctors, and good medical facilities provides a potentially rich source of developmental ideas and a testing ground for equipment developments. In addition, the medical research position in Israel should assist in creating a better market climate for Israeli medical equipment.
>
> For support of a teaching device industry, Israel can draw upon its rich and varied experience in youth movement work; in training of immigrants of many backgrounds, particularly in language: and in the special program for training Africans and Asians. This experience provides a large potential reservoir of sound ideas for a wide range of general and special application.[2]

It was shown in Chapter III that the market position of high-cost producers located in a large market is protected against competition from foreign low-cost producers when the differential between export and domestic marketing expenses is substantial. When such a situation exists it is conceivable that the high-cost producer will be able to compete with the low-cost producer, even in the latter's domestic market, and even though the latter enjoys a potential competitive edge in both manufacturing and marketing: denied access to the large export markets, the potential low-cost producer is saddled with fixed outlays which he is unable to spread over a sufficient number of units to reduce average costs to a competitive level.

The 'D' countries, which, by definition, have small domestic markets, may find themselves in such a predicament, especially in those cases where capital outlays per unit saleable in the domestic market are high. The 'A' countries, by contrast, benefit from such situations, even when local production factors such as labour are comparatively high-priced, because of their large domestic markets, which enable manufacturers to reduce unit costs. These markets are, to some extent, protected against foreign competition by differ-

---

[1] The following product lines were recommended in the report: teaching devices, test and measuring equipment, medical equipment, communication equipment, Hi-Fi equipment, printed circuitry, control systems. None of the above products belongs to the mature phase of the product cycle. See Stanford Research Institute, *A Study of the Potential for Development of an Electronics Industry in Israel* (Menlo Park, 1962), p. 32.

[2] Ibid., p. 33.

ential marketing costs. Since the differential tends to grow inversely with maturity, the countries most likely to be penalized by it are the 'D' countries, whose competitive strength was shown to be in first-phase products.

The next section discusses the view that the multi-national business firm is the instrument most suitable, under present conditions, to minimize the substantial cost disadvantage from which exporters of new products suffer, and to enable them to effectively tackle the problem of foreign entry.

E. THE EXPORT POTENTIAL OF MULTI-NATIONAL COMPANIES

Historically, multi-national companies fulfilled an important function in developing outlets for exports from the countries in which they operated. These exports were, however, limited as a rule to a small group of products: raw materials such as oil and iron ore, or agricultural commodities such as bananas and sugar. The investors frequently maintained a strong market position in their home country, and their investment was export-oriented from the outset. Traditional foreign investments were intended by their owners to replenish depleted natural resources or to obtain supplies which were altogether unavailable in their native countries.[1] By contrast, many of the more recent investments in foreign countries were made for the purpose of securing a market position (previously gained by exports) which was threatened by a rise of import duties and other trade restrictions, or by the local establishment of rival firms.[2]

Comparatively little attention has been given to the role which such companies can play in developing export markets for manufactured goods. Their presence in both the importing and the exporting countries provides them with numerous advantages denied to the traditional exporter who is physically remote from his market. Face-to-face communications can be maintained regularly with the customers when necessary. Essential service functions which the exporter must entrust to an agent can be

[1] See R. Nurkse, *Patterns of Trade and Development* (Oxford University Press, New York, 1961).

[2] See for example L. Gordon and E. L. Grommers, *United States Manufacturing Investment in Brazil* (Division of Research, Graduate School of Business Administration, Harvard University, Boston, 1962).

performed directly by the manufacturer's firm. Competitive developments are more likely to be monitored and communicated to the associated firms, and to be acted upon with minimum delay. This is not to say that serious inter-company communication problems may not exist or that breakdowns in the communication channels between the firm's constituent parts will not occur. These problems, however, are remediable by suitable administrative action. On the other hand, the difficulties faced by the traditional exporter arise from the fact that essential aspects of the marketing function are performed by independent organizations whose interests do not necessarily coincide with his own. When the exporter establishes his own marketing organization in the importing country, in order to secure adequate information and to be able to provide services at acceptable standards, he is likely to run into problems of scale and costly duplication of personnel and facilities, as in the case of the Israeli crystals manufacturer discussed in the previous chapter.

Consider for example how this same manufacturer could fare, had he been a part of a multi-national company engaged in manufacturing and marketing both in Israel and in the U.S. Crystal supplies could be obtained by the U.S. branch at prices representing substantial savings over the manufacturing costs of the local competitors.[1] The Israeli branch on its part need not have faced the formidable marketing problems which hamper the traditional exporter. Its output could be marketed by a firm which to all intents and purposes was local. It would have access to the latest market intelligence and available research findings, which would be communicated to it without delay. Research and development work could be conducted in the country where best results could be obtained for least cost. Production could similarly be allocated between the various branches as desired. The Israeli branch could be asked to manufacture parts and components containing crystals for the purpose of incorporating them into instruments or sub-assemblies produced in the U.S. Such flexibility is surely denied to independent companies, which have to deal with each other at arm's length, especially when they are separated from each other by many thousands of miles.

Operating within the framework of an international company the exporter is, in summary, competing on practically equal terms

---

[1] It will be recalled that delivered costs of Israel-made crystals amount to no more than 70 per cent of the production costs of the U.S. manufacturers.

with the local manufacturer in all matters concerning sales, services, and communication with the market. He can adopt the most effective marketing strategies, and pay for them no more than his local competitors would.[1]

Small countries in particular may benefit from the presence of international companies in their midst. Their domestic markets, as well as economic and scientific resources, are frequently too small to allow them to operate advanced industries on an optimal scale, as was shown in the preceding section. Multi-national enterprises may enable them to supplement their meagre resources with those of other nations and to overcome the disadvantage of small scale.

It is inconceivable, for example, that the Swiss pharmaceutical industry could have attained its present prominence had it not developed a world-wide network of subsidiaries. The industry could hardly have maintained its strong, world-wide market position for long by relying on export sales alone, if only because of the narrow economic and scientific base from which it was operating. Pharmaceuticals as a rule have a short life-span, and manufacturers must develop new products continuously in order to maintain their competitive strength. Having direct access to a huge market and to a large number of hospitals, universities, medical research institutions, and, above all, to a sizeable pool of competent scientists, U.S. manufacturers would undoubtedly have caught up with their Swiss competitors in the continuous race for new product development and consequently displaced them in the world markets.

The only strategy which the Swiss could adopt in order to avoid slipping behind was to establish their own research and manufacturing facilities in several foreign centres, including the U.S.

---

[1] Kindleberger makes the following comment about the relationship between international trade and the administrative framework within which it is being conducted.

Disarticulated firms working through highly organized markets are effective in the distribution of standardized products, the decentralized responsibility for decision-making for production on one hand and for selling on the other results in efficiency. When the character of products is changing, however, vertical integration can play a role in insuring that the producers and customer understand exactly how to adjust the relative needs of the one against the varying costs of the other. . . . The merchant system has lasted a long time in British industry, and is even today blamed for the lag in British exports in such lines as machine tools. By contrast, in the U.S. the rise of the national corporation after the development of the railroads led to a change in the institutional pattern in which the marketing function was taken back from the wholesaler into the enlarged corporation when it sold on a national rather than on regional lines.

C. P. Kindleberger, 'Protected Markets and Economic Growth', in Joint Economic Committee, *Factors Affecting the United States Balance of Payments* (Washington, Government Printing Office, 1962), p. 165.

By adopting this policy, a Swiss-based drug company, Ciba, is in the position to challenge 'American Pfizer's position as largest in the world'.[1] Other companies, such as Geigy and Hoffman-La Roche, have similarly attained considerable international prominence, and have maintained their position amongst the world's highest-ranking pharmaceutical manufacturers.

A similar strategy paid off handsomely in the case of Philips, the well-known Dutch electronics company. By maintaining research laboratories in the countries where the best talents could be obtained, and operating manufacturing facilities in the principal industrial centres of the world, the company succeeded in establishing itself as one of the world's leading electronics companies. This leadership position could have hardly been acquired, let alone maintained for long, had Philips confined its production and research to Holland. Philips' world-wide activities benefited not only its shareholders but the Dutch economy as a whole. The international scope of the company's operations was surely instrumental in establishing Holland as an electronics centre whose importance is more than proportional to the country's size and economic resources, as the following paragraph indicates:

Its world empire includes plants in thirty countries and marketing firms in 56; sales have tripled since 1956, and Philips hopes to be in a position soon to challenge the Radio Corporation of America for third place in the world in the electronics field ... This single company accounts for an *eighth*[2] of all Holland's industrial exports, it has 63 Dutch factories and 80,000 workers....[3]

Failure to 'go international' may have been at least partly responsible for the relative decline of the Swiss watch industry in the world's markets. High-quality craftsmanship combined with technological superiority enabled the industry to secure a position of unrivalled supremacy in the world markets during the second quarter of the present century. The Swiss sought to prevent the development of rival industries abroad by prohibiting the export of watch-making equipment, expecting thus to force the rest of the world to depend permanently on Swiss watches.

Lulled into a false sense of security, the manufacturers failed to modernize their production and distribution methods. When

[1] H. Martyn, *International Business* (London, The Free Press of Glencoe, 1964), p. 46.
[2] My italics.
[3] *The Economist*, 6 March, 1965.

Japanese and American manufacturers succeeded in bridging the technological gap by developing their own watch-making equipment, they managed to capture a considerable share of the market from the Swiss. Had the latter been encouraged to establish manufacturing subsidiaries abroad, they might have become prominent in the national industries of several countries. Their technological superiority and business experience could have enabled them to continue leading the world in the development of new production techniques and marketing concepts instead of following reluctantly in the footsteps of their foreign competitors.[1]

The experience of the Swiss and the Dutch shows that by combining the resources of several geographically dispersed units, and by serving a number of national markets, international companies can help small economies to overcome the disadvantage of small scale. They can also provide a framework which is most suitable for the transmission of technology, market intelligence, and goods between countries. Above all, they may be instrumental in accelerating the development of new, export-oriented industries in countries where they did not previously exist. The history of the Swiss watch industry indicates that failure to invest abroad may be as costly as a bad investment decision, though the costs, admittedly, are more difficult to gauge.

F. CONCLUSIONS

The product-cycle model presented in this study is predicated upon the proposition that comparative advantage is not a static phenomenon which remains constant over time. One of the model's major premises is that a country which has a strong competitive position in a particular industry at a given point in time may well lose this position when the industry enters into a new phase. Failure to recognize the dynamic nature of comparative advantage may lead policy-makers concerned with the enhancement of their country's export potential to adopt policies which go counter to its long-term interests. Such policies may lock up capital, labour, and other scarce resources in enterprises which should long have been abandoned, and may lead to the neglect of advantageous export opportunities.

---

[1] For a detailed account of the history of the watch industry, see the case series on the world watch industry published by the Harvard Graduate School of Business Administration.

By viewing their competitive potential within the framework of a dynamic comparative advantage model, manufacturers in the advanced countries might be able to anticipate the decline of their competitive strength in those products which are approaching the mature phase of the cycle. An early diagnosis of this kind might leave them ample time to transfer resources invested in existing industries into newer ones, where they might expect to manufacture on a competitive basis for some time to come.

Government planners and individual entrepreneurs in the less developed countries might similarly benefit by taking cognizance of the dynamic nature of comparative advantage. The model suggests that their advantage lies in industries whose technology has reached a sufficient degree of stability to be exportable to countries where engineers, skilled labourers, and scientists are scarce. Early identification of such industries might enable the pioneer (among the less developed countries) to secure a hold on the export markets in advance of potential competitors.

The model emphasizes the important role which the marketing function and marketing costs play in determining international competitiveness. The importance of marketing costs is not due only to their absolute or relative level, which at times may be quite high; their major significance lies in the fact that the costs of the exporters are, as a rule, higher than those of their domestic competitors. The difference between domestic and export marketing costs was shown to increase inversely with the maturity of the products in question. This fact hinders, in particular, exporters in the small developed countries, whose competitive strength is in new products.

Finally, some of the disadvantages suffered by manufacturers in the small developed countries might be offset by the establishment of multi-national business firms, or by association with existing ones. The presence of multi-national firms in different countries facilitates the effective transmission of market information, technology, specifications, research results, and goods between the geographically dispersed component units. Their ability to combine and shuffle resources of several enterprises located in different countries enables the multi-national firms to benefit to some extent from the economies of scale and external economies which only proximity to large markets confers.

INDEX

PRINTED IN GREAT BRITAIN BY
THE SALISBURY PRESS LTD., SALISBURY

Date Due